822.33
W 1
Yale
part 1

Shak Y0-CVJ-950

The first part of
King Henry the Fourth.

DATE DUE

WITHDRAWN

The Yale Shakespeare.

THE FIRST PART OF KING HENRY THE FOURTH

NEW EDITION REVISED BY
TUCKER BROOKE

This new edition of THE FIRST PART OF KING HENRY THE FOURTH and a number of other plays in THE YALE SHAKESPEARE have been prepared by TUCKER BROOKE who has used, added to, and brought up to date the work of the previous editors whose names appear with his in the separate volumes.

The Yale Shakespeare.

The First Part of King Henry the Fourth

EDITED BY TUCKER BROOKE

AND

SAMUEL B. HEMINGWAY

New Haven and London
Yale University Press

Copyright, 1917, 1947, by Yale University Press

FIRST PUBLISHED, SEPTEMBER 1917
REVISED EDITION, AUGUST 1947

Sixth printing, February 1964

Printed in the United States of America

All rights reserved in the editorial contributions to this edition, which may not be reprinted, in whole or in part, except by written permission of the publishers.

Library of Congress catalog card number: 48–250

PUBLISHED ON THE FUND
GIVEN TO THE YALE UNIVERSITY PRESS IN 1917
BY THE MEMBERS OF THE
KINGSLEY TRUST ASSOCIATION
(SCROLL AND KEY SOCIETY OF YALE COLLEGE)
TO COMMEMORATE THE SEVENTY-FIFTH ANNIVERSARY
OF THE FOUNDING OF THE SOCIETY

CONTENTS

Shakespeare and the *Textus Receptus*	6
The Text	13
Notes	134
Appendix A. Sources	152
Appendix B. History of the Play	157
Index of Words Glossed	163

SHAKESPEARE
AND THE *TEXTUS RECEPTUS**

It is rather paradoxical that Spenser, who 'writ no language,' as his contemporary Jonson asserted, yet persists for us—when some rather simple allowances are made for odd rime and grammar—as a well of Elizabethan English undefiled; whereas Shakespeare, who wrote racy, colloquial, and sometimes flamboyant Elizabethan, confronts the modern reader in a form which often gives him the aspect of an eighteenth-century classic. The late Dr. McKerrow was not greatly exaggerating when he wrote in an annual Shakespeare lecture of the British Academy:

> In spite of the work of the last 150 years, Shakespeare, as he is known in the literature, not only of our own country, but of the world, is still in the main the Shakespeare of Rowe, Pope, Theobald, Johnson, and the other eighteenth-century editors.

McKerrow saw in this the praise of Rowe and his influential successors. Without detracting from the greatness or historic usefulness of their services, I would ask whether it is not time to liberate the poet more completely than has yet been done from the strong web which so remarkably attaches him to the sensibilities, methods, and ideas of a century as remote from his own age as from ours.

The quality about Shakespeare's works which troubled learned readers a century after his death—and troubled them more than his Gothic 'bombast'—was the sheer difficulty of understanding him.

Dr. McKerrow has quoted Francis Atterbury's confession to Pope in 1721:

---

* The following essay by Mr. Brooke was read at a meeting of the Modern Language Association in 1945.

Shakespeare and the *Textus Receptus* 7

> I have found time to read some parts of Shakespeare, which I was least acquainted with. I protest to you, in a hundred places I cannot construe him: I do not understand him. The hardest part of Chaucer is more intelligible to me than some of those scenes, not merely through the faults of the edition, but the obscurity of the writer, for obscure he is.

Obscure he often is, certainly; and it is a mark of virtue, no doubt, that Pope and his brethren proceeded, with the downright earnestness that distinguished their great age, to make Shakespeare talk sense. But it is discreditable to us, who know so much more of Shakespeare's language and range of ideas, and are fortified on all sides by dictionaries, texts, concordances, grammars, and manuals undreamed of in the past, that we continue to give out as genuine, or at least unimprovable, Shakespeare what is too often only the desperate guess of a gravelled eighteenth-century editor.

The sledded Polacks in *Hamlet*, the tired Ingener in *Othello*, the 'lym' or lime-hound who joins the procession of dogs in *Lear* (III.vii.74) on the invitation of Hanmer, the very, very pea-jock or peacock to which Hamlet compares his uncle, the remarkable ostriches that with their wings baited like eagles having lately bathed (*1 Henry IV*. IV.i.98) seem to be mainly products of the eighteenth-century desire for clear and concrete figure. One could make quite a list of flora and fauna in the plays which the poet would never have recognized, though they still pass almost unquestioned.

As everybody knows, the division of scenes is largely, and their location almost entirely, the work of the early editors. Yet, with hardly a question, we read and teach and reprint the plays as if these things were essentials of Shakespeare's art, though they sometimes distort his dramatic purpose, and often totally misrepresent the theater for which he was writing. Only one or two modern editors, and probably not many more teachers, will begin the fourth act of *Hamlet* at any point except the absurd one that a late seventeenth-century actors' quarto curiously hit upon. No critic or editor known to me appears to doubt that the first scene of Act Third of *1 Henry IV* takes place at Bangor, where Hotspur, Worcester, Mortimer, and Glendower, with wives and all their followers, are supposed to be the house guests of the Archdeacon. No Elizabethan could have imagined such a social absurdity, and of course nothing in the text hints at it; but Theobald misunderstood a passage in Holinshed, and no questions were ever asked. In the same play Shakespeare's wonderful pageant of the opening of the Battle of Shrewsbury is destroyed, both for the reader and on the stage, because Pope (and everybody after him) split it at the point of closest cohesion into two scenes. In *Antony and Cleopatra* this kind of thing has proceeded so far that the play is at times nearly as unreadable as it is, on this basis, unactable.

Everybody knows that Pope purified a great deal of Shakespeare's meter, and was abetted by his followers in this dull game. Here—as also in the case of the scenes and speeches which the eighteenth century omitted outright, or degraded to footnotes, because in their view unworthy of a gentleman and a Shakespeare—recent editors have repaired much damage. But it is remarkable how many passages of fine honest prose, like Lear's great speech beginning 'Ay, every inch a king' still, in all our editions, hobble along on Popian stilts as alleged verse.

It was, of course, the Folio text that the early editors took as their point of departure. It was all that some of them knew, and it is all we yet have to depend on for half the plays. Yet, where the Folio can be compared with an honest Quarto text, one generally finds that it presents a histrionic sophistication of the original. It has myriads of capital letters which an Elizabethan would not have used, and which were an irresistible invitation to the age of Pope to turn plain homespun nouns into baroque allegories and personifications. It has thousands of colons which had the effect of gumming disparate sentences together into something presumably rich and strange, but unintelligible to the common mind. One of the very hardest jobs for the teacher of to-day is to un-stick these compounds and penetrate to the original meaning after Dr. Johnson has employed his incomparable dialectic upon the amalgam. One hates to do it, of course; for the first effect is disappointment at discovering that the poet is only talking sense and not metaphysic. In this matter of punctuation, candles should be lighted in memory of the late Professor Kittredge, who of all moderns appears to have made the most courageous effort to punctuate the works of Shakespeare according to their plain and pure meaning.

In wording also the Folio often over-paints the Shakespearean lily. It was the Folio that threw that apple of discord among the critics, Othello's 'upon this hint I spake'; and the other about the time of scorn's 'slow and moving finger'—two fruits, I am sure, not plucked from Shakespeare's garden. It is the Folio that somewhat mouthily expands Othello's simple outburst (as the Quarto has it), 'But yet the pity of it, Iago, the pity!' into 'But yet the pity of it, Iago! O Iago! The pity of it, Iago!' and heightens his invocation of the mortal engines whose *wide* throats the Immortal Jove's *great* clamors counterfeit into *rude* throats and *dread* clamors. The Folio causes Iago to come in (V.ii.317) not 'in the *nick*' but 'in the *interim*.' It kills Oswald in *Lear* with a possibly poetic, but quite unknown, weapon, a 'ballow' instead of a plain batoon; and in scores of other places it shows that somebody was improving on the old poet long before the Restoration adapters took up the task.

The process went on like the Pontic sea through the sequence of the Folios and into the eighteenth century, and, curiously, it has felt no retiring ebb in more recent times. The Shakespeare that we still want for our money is the Shakespeare that Johnson edited, that Kemble and Kean and Irving recited, which is, of course, the embellished eighteenth-century Shakespeare. It will be the business of the next generation to accustom our literary palates to the simpler fare that the man of Stratford gave the Elizabethans.

The map opposite shows the principal towns, rivers, etc., mentioned in The First Part of King Henry the Fourth.

[THE ACTORS' NAMES

KING HENRY THE FOURTH
HENRY, PRINCE OF WALES } his sons
PRINCE JOHN OF LANCASTER
RICHARD SCROOP, Archbishop of York
EDMUND MORTIMER, Earl of March
RALPH NEVILLE, Earl of Westmorland
HENRY PERCY, Earl of Northumberland
THOMAS PERCY, Earl of Worcester, his brother
HENRY PERCY, surnamed Hotspur, Northumberland's son
ARCHIBALD, Earl of Douglas
OWEN GLENDOWER, a Welsh chieftain
SIR JOHN FALSTAFF
SIR WALTER BLUNT
SIR RICHARD VERNON
SIR MICHAEL, attendant on the Archbishop of York
EDWARD POINS
PETO   } companions of the Prince of Wales and
GADSHILL   Falstaff
BARDOLPH
FRANCIS, a tavern drawer
LADY KATE PERCY, wife of Hotspur and sister of Mortimer
LADY MORTIMER, wife of Mortimer and daughter of Glendower
MISTRESS QUICKLY, hostess of the Boar's Head Tavern
Lords, Officers, Sheriff of London, Vintner, an inn chamberlain, two carriers, travellers, and attendants
SCENE: Various parts of England and Wales.]

The First Part of Henry the Fourth

With the Life and Death of Henry, Surnamed Hotspur

ACT FIRST

SCENE FIRST

[*Westminster. The King's Palace*]

Enter the King, Lord John of Lancaster, Earl of Westmorland, with others.

King. So shaken as we are, so wan with care,
Find we a time for frighted peace to pant,
And breathe short-winded accents of new broils
To be commenc'd in stronds afar remote. 4
No more the thirsty entrance of this soil
Shall daub her lips with her own children's blood,
No more shall trenching war channel her fields,
Nor bruise her flowerets with the armed hoofs 8
Of hostile paces. Those opposed eyes,
Which like the meteors of a troubled heaven,
All of one nature, of one substance bred,
Did lately meet in the intestine shock 12
And furious close of civil butchery,
Shall now in mutual well-beseeming ranks
March all one way, and be no more oppos'd

---

4 stronds: *coasts; cf. n.*   5 Cf. *n.*
7 trenching: *trench-digging*   channel: *make channels in*
12 intestine: *internal, civil*   13 close: *grapple*
14 mutual well-beseeming ranks: *ranks which have, most properly, a common interest*

14 The First Part of Henry the Fourth

Against acquaintance, kindred, and allies. 16
The edge of war, like an ill-sheathed knife,
No more shall cut his master. Therefore, friends,
As far as to the sepulcher of Christ—
Whose soldier now, under whose blessed cross 20
We are impressed and engag'd to fight—
Forthwith a power of English shall we levy,
Whose arms were moulded in their mothers' womb,
To chase these pagans in those holy fields, 24
Over whose acres walk'd those blessed feet
Which fourteen hundred years ago were nail'd
For our advantage on the bitter cross.
But this our purpose now is twelve month old, 28
And bootless 'tis to tell you we will go.
Therefore we meet not now. Then let me hear
Of you, my gentle cousin Westmorland,
What yesternight our council did decree 32
In forwarding this dear expedience.

West. My liege, this haste was hot in question,
And many limits of the charge set down
But yesternight, when all athwart there came 36
A post from Wales, loaden with heavy news,
Whose worst was that the noble Mortimer,
Leading the men of Herefordshire to fight
Against the irregular and wild Glendower, 40
Was by the rude hands of that Welshman taken,

---

21 impressed: *compelled into service*   26 Cf. *n.*
28 Cf. *n.*   29 bootless: *useless*
33 dear expedience: *important expedition*
34 hot in question: *in hot debate*
35 limits of the charge: *implementing provisions*
36 athwart: *crossing this plan*
38 Mortimer; cf. *n.*   40 irregular: *lawless*

Act I, Scene 1

A thousand of his people butchered,
Upon whose dead corpes there was such misuse,
Such beastly shameless transformation　　　　　　44
By those Welshwomen done, as may not be
(Without much shame) re-told or spoken of.

　King. It seems then that the tidings of this broil
Brake off our business for the Holy Land.　　　　48

　West. This match'd with other did, my gracious lord,
For more uneven and unwelcome news
Came from the North, and thus it did import:
On Holy-rood day, the gallant Hotspur there,　　　52
Young Harry Percy, and brave Archibold,
That ever-valiant and approved Scot,
At Holmedon met,
Where they did spend a sad and bloody hour,　　　56
As by discharge of their artillery
And shape of likelihood the news was told;
For he that brought them in the very heat
And pride of their contention did take horse,　　　60
Uncertain of the issue any way.

　King. Here is a dear, a true, industrious friend,
Sir Walter Blunt, new lighted from his horse,
Stain'd with the variation of each soil　　　　　　64
Betwixt that Holmedon and this seat of ours;
And he hath brought us smooth and welcome news.
The Earl of Douglas is discomfited,
Ten thousand bold Scots, two and twenty knights,　68
Balk'd in their own blood did Sir Walter see

---

43 corpes: *bodies*　　　　　　49 match'd: *joined*
50 uneven: *disconcerting*　　52 Holy-rood day; *cf. n.*
53 Young Harry Percy; *cf. n.*　54 approved: *well-tried*
57, 58 *Cf. n.*　　　　　　　　69 Balk'd: *piled up*

16   The First Part of Henry the Fourth

On Holmedon's plains. Of prisoners Hotspur took
Mordake Earl of Fife, and eldest son
To beaten Douglas, and the Earl of Athol, 72
Of Murray, Angus, and Menteith.
And is not this an honorable spoil?
A gallant prize? ha, cousin, is it not?
   West. In faith, 76
It is a conquest for a prince to boast of.
   King. Yea, there thou mak'st me sad, and mak'st me sin
In envy, that my Lord Northumberland
Should be the father to so blest a son, 80
A son who is the theme of honor's tongue,
Amongst a grove the very straightest plant,
Who is sweet Fortune's minion and her pride;
Whilst I by looking on the praise of him 84
See riot and dishonor stain the brow
Of my young Harry. O that it could be prov'd
That some night-tripping fairy had exchang'd
In cradle-clothes our children where they lay, 88
And call'd mine Percy, his Plantagenet.
Then would I have his Harry, and he mine.
But let him from my thoughts. What think you, coz,
Of this young Percy's pride? The prisoners 92
Which he in this adventure hath surpris'd
To his own use he keeps, and sends me word
I shall have none but Mordake Earl of Fife.
   West. This is his uncle's teaching. This is Worcester,
Malevolent to you in all aspécts, 97

---

71 Mordake; *cf. n.*
83 minion: *darling*
91 coz: *cousin, used by the sovereign in addressing any nobleman*
91–95 *Cf. n.* 97 *Cf. n.*

Act I, Scene 1

Which makes him prune himself, and bristle up
The crest of youth against your dignity.
  King. But I have sent for him to answer this.   100
And for this cause a while we must neglect
Our holy purpose to Jerusalem.
Cousin, on Wednesday next our council we
Will hold at Windsor. So inform the lords: 104
But come yourself with speed to us again,
For more is to be said and to be done
Than out of anger can be uttered.
  West. I will, my liege.   *Exeunt.*

SCENE SECOND

[Westminster. A Public Waiting Room at Court]

Enter Prince of Wales and Sir John Falstaff.

  Fal. Now Hal, what time of day is it, lad?
  Prince. Thou art so fat-witted with drinking of old sack, and unbuttoning thee after supper, and sleeping upon benches after noon, that thou hast forgotten to demand that truly which thou wouldst truly know. What a devil hast thou to do with the time of the day? Unless hours were cups of sack, and minutes capons, and clocks the tongues of bawds, and dials the signs of leaping-houses, and the blessed sun himself a fair hot wench in flame-color'd taffeta, I see no

---

98 Which: *who*   107 uttered; *cf. n.*
Scene Second. S. d.; *cf. n.*
3 sack: *sweet Spanish wine*   9 leaping-houses: *brothels*

reason why thou shouldst be so superfluous to demand the time of the day.

Fal. Indeed you come near me now, Hal; for we that take purses go by the moon and the seven stars, and not by Phœbus, he, 'that wandering knight so fair.' And I prithee, sweet wag, when thou art a king, as God save thy Grace—Majesty I should say, for grace thou wilt have none—

Prince. What, none?

Fal. No, by my troth; not so much as will serve to be prologue to an egg and butter.

Prince. Well, how then? come roundly, roundly.

Fal. Marry then, sweet wag, when thou art king let not us that are squires of the night's body be called thieves of the day's beauty. Let us be Diana's foresters, gentlemen of the shade, minions of the moon; and let men say we be men of good government, being governed as the sea is, by our noble and chaste mistress the moon, under whose countenance we steal.

Prince. Thou sayest well, and it holds well too; for the fortune of us that are the moon's men doth ebb and flow like the sea, being governed as the sea is by the moon. As for proof now: a purse of gold most resolutely snatched on Monday night and most dissolutely spent on Tuesday morning; got with swear-

11 superfluous: *supererogatory*
15 wandering knight; *cf. n.*
21 egg and butter: *scrambled egg*
22 roundly: *plainly, to the point*
23 Marry: *well (originally an oath)*
25 Diana's: *the moon's*
26 minions: *favorites*

14 *Cf. n.*
17–30 *Cf. n.*

Act I, Scene 2

ing 'Lay by!' and spent with crying 'Bring in!' now in as low an ebb as the foot of the ladder, and by and by in as high a flow as the ridge of the gallows.

Fal. By the Lord thou sayest true, lad. And is not my hostess of the tavern a most sweet wench?

Prince. As the honey of Hybla, my old lad of the castle. And is not a buff jerkin a most sweet robe of durance?

Fal. How now, how now, mad wag! what, in thy quips and thy quiddities? what a plague have I to do with a buff jerkin?

Prince. Why, what a pox have I to do with my hostess of the tavern?

Fal. Well, thou hast called her to a reckoning many a time and oft.

Prince. Did I ever call for thee to pay thy part?

Fal. No, I'll give thee thy due, thou hast paid all there.

Prince. Yea, and elsewhere, so far as my coin would stretch; and where it would not, I have used my credit.

Fal. Yea, and so used it that were it not here apparent that thou art heir-apparent—but I prithee sweet wag, shall there be gallows standing in England when thou art king and resolution thus fubbed

---

37 'Lay by': *address of highwaymen to their victims*   'Bring in': *a call for wine*
42 honey of Hybla: *Sicilian honey*   lad of the castle; *cf. Appendix B*
43,44 buff jerkin . . . durance; *cf. n.*
44 durance: *a stuff noted for its durability*
46 quips: *jests*   quiddities: *subtleties, puns*
61 resolution: *enterprise*   fubbed: *hampered*

The First Part of Henry the Fourth

as it is with the rusty curb of old Father Antic the Law? Do not thou, when thou art king, hang a thief.

Prince. No, thou shalt.

Fal. Shall I? O rare! By the Lord I'll be a brave judge.

Prince. Thou judgest false already. I mean thou shalt have the hanging of the thieves, and so become a rare hangman.

Fal. Well, Hal, well; and in some sort it jumps with my humor as well as waiting in the court, I can tell you.

Prince. For obtaining of suits?

Fal. Yea, for obtaining of suits, whereof the hangman hath no lean wardrobe. 'Sblood I am as melancholy as a gib cat, or a lugged bear.

Prince. Or an old lion, or a lover's lute.

Fal. Yea, or the drone of a Lincolnshire bagpipe.

Prince. What sayest thou to a hare, or the melancholy of Moorditch?

Fal. Thou hast the most unsavory similes, and art indeed the most comparative, rascalliest, sweet young prince! But Hal, I prithee trouble me no more with vanity. I would to God thou and I knew where a commodity of good names were to be bought.

62 Antic: *buffoon*   66 brave: *fine*
71 jumps: *agrees*   72 humor: *inclination*
74 obtaining of suits: *the clothes of the criminal were the hangman's perquisite*
76 'Sblood: *God's blood*
77 gib cat: *tom cat*   lugged bear: *bear led by a rope*
80 hare; *cf. n.*   81 Moorditch; *cf. n.*
83 comparative: *witty, critical*
86 commodity: *second-hand supply*

Act I, Scene 2 21

An old lord of the council rated me the other day in the street about you, sir, but I marked him not; and yet he talked very wisely, but I regarded him not; and yet he talked wisely, and in the street too. 90

Prince. Thou didst well, for wisdom cries out in the streets and no man regards it.

Fal. O thou hast damnable iteration, and art indeed able to corrupt a saint. Thou hast done much harm upon me, Hal, God forgive thee for it! Before I knew thee, Hal, I knew nothing, and now am I, if a man should speak truly, little better than one of the wicked. I must give over this life, and I will give it over. By the Lord, an I do not, I am a villain. I'll be damned for never a king's son in Christendom. 100

Prince. Where shall we take a purse tomorrow, Jack?

Fal. 'Zounds! where thou wilt, lad, I'll make one. An I do not, call me villain and baffle me. 104

Prince. I see a good amendment of life in thee: from praying to purse-taking.

Fal. Why, Hal, 'tis my vocation, Hal. 'Tis no sin for a man to labor in his vocation. 108

Enter Poins.

Poins! Now shall we know if Gadshill have set a match. O, if men were to be saved by merit, what hole in hell were hot enough for him? This is the most omnipotent villain that ever cried 'Stand!' to a true man. 113

93 damnable iteration; *cf. n.*   103 'Zounds: *God's wounds*
104 baffle: *hang by the heels (a punishment inflicted on recreant knights)*
109 Gadshill; *cf. n.*   set a match: *planned a robbery*

22   The First Part of Henry the Fourth

Prince. Good morrow, Ned.

Poins. Good morrow, sweet Hal. What says Monsieur Remorse? What says Sir John Sack-and-Sugar, Jack? How agrees the devil and thee about thy soul, that thou soldest him on Good-Friday last for a cup of Madeira and a cold capon's leg? 119

Prince. Sir John stands to his word. The devil shall have his bargain, for he was never yet a breaker of proverbs. He will give the devil his due.

Poins. Then art thou damned for keeping thy word with the devil. 124

Prince. Else he had been damned for cozening the devil.

Poins. But my lads, my lads, to-morrow morning, by four o'clock early at Gadshill there are pilgrims going to Canterbury with rich offerings, and traders riding to London with fat purses. I have vizards for you all, you have horses for yourselves. Gadshill lies to-night in Rochester, I have bespoke supper to-morrow night in Eastcheap; we may do it as secure as sleep. If you will go, I will stuff your purses full of crowns. If you will not, tarry at home and be hanged. 136

Fal. Hear ye, Yedward, if I tarry at home and go not, I'll hang you for going.

Poins. You will, chops?

Fal. Hal, wilt thou make one? 140

Prince. Who, I rob? I a thief? Not I, by my faith.

Fal. There's neither honesty, manhood, nor good

118, 119 Cf. *n.*
128 pilgrims; cf. *n.*
133 Eastcheap; cf. *n.*

125 cozening: *cheating*
130 vizards: *masks*
139 chops: *fat face*

Act I, Scene 2

fellowship in thee, nor thou cam'st not of the blood royal, if thou darest not stand for ten shillings. 144

Prince. Well then, once in my days I'll be a madcap.

Fal. Why, that's well said.

Prince. Well, come what will, I'll tarry at home.

Fal. By the Lord, I'll be a traitor then, when thou art king. 150

Prince. I care not.

Poins. Sir John, I prithee leave the prince and me alone. I will lay him down such reasons for this adventure that he shall go. 154

Fal. Well God give thee the spirit of persuasion and him the ears of profiting, that what thou speakest may move, and what he hears may be believed, that the true prince may (for recreation sake) prove a false thief, for the poor abuses of the time want countenance. Farewell. You shall find me in Eastcheap. 161

Prince. Farewell the latter spring! Farewell Allhallown summer! [*Exit Falstaff.*]

Poins. Now my good sweet honey lord, ride with us to-morrow. I have a jest to execute, that I cannot manage alone. Falstaff, Bardolph, Peto, and Gadshill shall rob those men that we have already waylaid. Yourself and I will not be there. And when they have the booty, if you and I do not rob them, cut this head off from my shoulders. 170

---

144 stand for ten shillings; *cf. n.*
145 Well then, *etc.; cf. n.*   162 the latter spring; *cf. n.*
162, 163 Allhallown summer: *All Saints' summer; cf. n.*
166 Bardolph, Peto; *cf. n.*
167 waylaid: *lain in wait for, snared*

Prince. How shall we part with them in setting forth?

Poins. Why, we will set forth before or after them, and appoint them a place of meeting, wherein it is at our pleasure to fail; and then will they adventure upon the exploit themselves, which they shall have no sooner achieved but we'll set upon them. 177

Prince. Yea but 'tis like that they will know us by our horses, by our habits, and by every other appointment to be ourselves. 180

Poins. Tut! our horses they shall not see, I'll tie them in the wood. Our vizards we will change after we leave them. And sirrah, I have cases of buckram for the nonce, to immask our noted outward garments. 185

Prince. Yea, but I doubt they will be too hard for us.

Poins. Well, for two of them, I know them to be as true-bred cowards as ever turned back; and for the third, if he fight longer than he sees reason, I'll forswear arms. The virtue of this jest will be the incomprehensible lies that this same fat rogue will tell us when we meet at supper: how thirty at least he fought with, what wards, what blows, what extremities he endured, and in the reproof of this lies the jest. 196

Prince. Well, I'll go with thee. Provide us all

179 habits: *clothes*   appointment: *equipment*
183 sirrah; *cf. n.*   cases of buckram: *cloaks of coarse linen*
184 for the nonce: *for the occasion*   noted: *well-known*
189, 190 the third; *cf. n.*
191 incomprehensible: *limitless*
194 wards: *guards in fencing*   195 reproof: *refutation*

Act I, Scene 2

things necessary, and meet me to-morrow night in
Eastcheap. There I'll sup. Farewell.
    Poins. Farewell, my lord.   *Exit Poins.*
    Prince. I know you all, and will awhile uphold   201
The unyok'd humor of your idleness.
Yet herein will I imitate the sun,
Who doth permit the base contagious clouds   204
To smother up his beauty from the world,
That when he please again to be himself,
Being wanted, he may be more wonder'd at
By breaking through the foul and ugly mists   208
Of vapors that did seem to strangle him.
If all the year were playing-holidays,
To sport would be as tedious as to work;
But when they seldom come, they wish'd for come,   212
And nothing pleaseth but rare accidents.
So when this loose behavior I throw off,
And pay the debt I never promised,
By how much better than my word I am,   216
By so much shall I falsify men's hopes,
And like bright metal on a sullen ground,
My reformation, glittering o'er my fault,
Shall show more goodly, and attract more eyes,   220
Than that which hath no foil to set it off.
I'll so offend, to make offence a skill,
Redeeming time when men think least I will.   *Exit.*

201–223 *Cf. n.*
202 unyok'd humor: *unrestrained caprice*
204 contagious: *pestilential*
213 accidents: *events not arising from routine*
218 sullen: *dull*

SCENE THIRD

[Windsor Castle]

Enter the King, Northumberland, Worcester, Hotspur, Sir Walter Blunt, with others.

King. My blood hath been too cold and temperate,
Unapt to stir at these indignities,
And you have found me; for accordingly
You tread upon my patience. But be sure   4
I will from henceforth rather be myself,
Mighty, and to be fear'd, than my condition,
Which hath been smooth as oil, soft as young down,
And therefore lost that title of respect,   8
Which the proud soul ne'er pays but to the proud.

Wor. Our house, my sovereign liege, little deserves
The scourge of greatness to be us'd on it,
And that same greatness too, which our own hands   12
Have holp to make so portly.

North. My lord—

King. Worcester, get thee gone, for I do see
Danger and disobedience in thine eye.   16
O sir, your presence is too bold and peremptory,
And majesty might never yet endure
The moody frontier of a servant brow.

Scene Third. Windsor Castle; *cf. n.*
3 found me: *guessed my character*
6 condition: *natural disposition*
8 lost: *hath lost*   13 portly: *stately*
19 moody: *angry*   frontier: *outworks of a fort (used figuratively)*

Act I, Scene 3

You have good leave to leave us. When we need 20
Your use and counsel we shall send for you.
                              Exit Worcester.
[*To Northumberland.*] You were about to speak.
  North.   Yea my good lord.
Those prisoners in your highness' name demanded,
Which Harry Percy here at Holmedon took, 24
Were, as he says, not with such strength denied
As is deliver'd to your majesty.
Either envy therefore, or misprision,
Is guilty of this fault, and not my son. 28
  Hot. My liege, I did deny no prisoners.
But I remember when the fight was done,
When I was dry with rage, and extreme toil,
Breathless and faint, leaning upon my sword, 32
Came there a certain lord, neat and trimly dress'd,
Fresh as a bridegroom, and his chin, new reap'd,
Show'd like a stubble-land at harvest-home.
He was perfumed like a milliner, 36
And 'twixt his finger and his thumb he held
A pouncet-box, which ever and anon
He gave his nose, and took't away again,
Who therewith angry, when it next came there 40
Took it in snuff, and still he smil'd and talk'd.
And as the soldiers bore dead bodies by,
He call'd them untaught knaves, unmannerly,
To bring a slovenly unhandsome corse 44
Betwixt the wind and his nobility.

---

26 deliver'd: *reported*
27 misprision: *misapprehension*   36 milliner; *cf. n.*
38 pouncet-box: *a perforated box for perfumes*
41 in snuff: *as an offence (with play on the word snuff)*

28   The First Part of Henry the Fourth

With many holiday and lady terms
He question'd me, amongst the rest demanded
My prisoners in your majesty's behalf.   48
I then, all smarting with my wounds being cold,
To be so pester'd with a popinjay,
Out of my grief and my impatience
Answer'd neglectingly, I know not what,   52
He should, or he should not, for he made me mad
To see him shine so brisk, and smell so sweet,
And talk so like a waiting-gentlewoman,
Of guns, and drums, and wounds—God save the mark!—
And telling me the sovereign'st thing on earth   57
Was parmaceti, for an inward bruise;
And that it was great pity, so it was,
This villainous saltpeter should be digg'd   60
Out of the bowels of the harmless earth,
Which many a good tall fellow had destroy'd
So cowardly, and but for these vile guns
He would himself have been a soldier.   64
This bald unjointed chat of his, my lord,
I answer'd indirectly, as I said,
And I beseech you, let not his report
Come current for an accusation   68
Betwixt my love and your high majesty.
   Blunt. The circumstance consider'd, good my lord,
What e'er Lord Harry Percy then had said
To such a person, and in such a place,   72

---

46 holiday and lady terms: *choice and ladylike expressions*
47 question'd: *chatted with*   50 popinjay: *parrot*
51 grief: *pain*   56 God save the mark: *cf. n.*
57 sovereign'st: *of supreme excellence*
58 parmaceti: *spermaceti, a substance found in whales*
62 tall: *valiant*

Act I, Scene 3

At such a time, with all the rest re-told,
May reasonably die, and never rise
To do him wrong, or any way impeach
What then he said, so he unsay it now. 76

King. Why yet he doth deny his prisoners,
But with proviso and exception,
That we at our own charge shall ransom straight
His brother-in-law, the foolish Mortimer, 80
Who, on my soul, hath wilfully betray'd
The lives of those that he did lead to fight
Against that great magician, damn'd Glendower,
Whose daughter, as we hear, that Earl of March 84
Hath lately married. Shall our coffers then
Be emptied, to redeem a traitor home?
Shall we buy treason, and indent with fears,
When they have lost and forfeited themselves? 88
No, on the barren mountains let him starve;
For I shall never hold that man my friend,
Whose tongue shall ask me for one penny cost
To ransom home revolted Mortimer. 92

Hot. Revolted Mortimer!
He never did fall off, my sovereign liege,
But by the chance of war. To prove that true
Needs no more but one tongue for all those wounds, 96
Those mouthed wounds which valiantly he took,
When on the gentle Severn's sedgy bank,
In single opposition hand to hand,

---

73 re-told: *that he has told over*
75 impeach: *call in question*
80 brother-in-law; *cf. n. on lines 145, 146*
84 Earl of March: *Mortimer*
87 indent: *bargain*   94 fall off: *desert*
97 mouthed wounds: *wounds that speak aloud*

He did confound the best part of an hour 100
In changing hardiment with great Glendower.
Three times they breath'd and three times did they drink,
Upon agreement, of swift Severn's flood,
Who then affrighted with their bloody looks, 104
Ran fearfully among the trembling reeds,
And hid his crisp head in the hollow bank,
Blood-stained with these valiant combatants.
Never did base and rotten policy 108
Color her working with such deadly wounds,
Nor never could the noble Mortimer
Receive so many, and all willingly.
Then let not him be slander'd with revolt. 112
 King. Thou dost belie him, Percy, thou dost belie him.
He never did encounter with Glendower.
I tell thee,
He durst as well have met the devil alone 116
As Owen Glendower for an enemy.
Art thou not asham'd? But sirrah, henceforth
Let me not hear you speak of Mortimer.
Send me your prisoners with the speediest means, 120
Or you shall hear in such a kind from me
As will displease you. My Lord Northumberland,
We license your departure with your son.
Send us your prisoners, or you will hear of it. 124
  Exit King [with Blunt and train].
 Hot. And if the devil come and roar for them
I will not send them. I will after straight

---

100 confound: *consume*
101 changing hardiment: *exchanging valor*
106 crisp: *curled, i.e., rippled*
109 Color: *disguise* 121 kind: *way*
125 And if: *even if* 126 straight: *immediately*

Act I, Scene 3

And tell him so, for I will ease my heart,
Albeit I make a hazard of my head. 128
 North. What? drunk with choler? stay, and pause
   awhile.
Here comes your uncle.

Enter Worcester.

 Hot.   Speak of Mortimer?
'Zounds I will speak of him! and let my soul
Want mercy if I do not join with him. 132
Yea on his part I'll empty all these veins,
And shed my dear blood, drop by drop in the dust,
But I will lift the down-trod Mortimer
As high in the air as this unthankful king, 136
As this ingrate and canker'd Bolingbroke.
 North. Brother, the king hath made your nephew mad.
 Wor. Who struck this heat up after I was gone?
 Hot. He will, forsooth, have all my prisoners. 140
And when I urg'd the ransom once again
Of my wife's brother, then his cheek look'd pale,
And on my face he turn'd an eye of death,
Trembling even at the name of Mortimer. 144
 Wor. I cannot blame him. Was not he proclaim'd
By Richard that dead is, the next of blood?
 North. He was. I heard the proclamation.
And then it was, when the unhappy king 148
(Whose wrongs in us God pardon) did set forth
Upon his Irish expedition;
From whence he, intercepted, did return

---

128 Albeit . . . hazard: *though at the risk*
129 choler: *anger*
137 canker'd: *malignant*   Bolingbroke; *cf. n.*
145, 146 *Cf. n.*   149 in us: *at our hands*

To be depos'd, and shortly murdered. 152
  Wor. And for whose death, we in the world's wide mouth
Live scandaliz'd and foully spoken of.
  Hot. But soft, I pray you, did King Richard then
Proclaim my brother Edmund Mortimer 156
Heir to the crown?
  North.   He did; myself did hear it.
  Hot. Nay, then I cannot blame his cousin king,
That wish'd him on the barren mountains starve.
But shall it be that you that set the crown 160
Upon the head of this forgetful man,
And for his sake wear the detested blot
Of murtherous subornation—shall it be,
That you a world of curses undergo, 164
Being the agents, or base second means,
The cords, the ladder, or the hangman rather—
O pardon me that I descend so low,
To show the line and the predicament 168
Wherein you range under this subtle king!—
Shall it for shame be spoken in these days,
Or fill up chronicles in time to come,
That men of your nobility and power 172
Did gage them both in an unjust behalf
(As both of you, God pardon it, have done)
To put down Richard, that sweet lovely rose,
And plant this thorn, this canker Bolingbroke? 176
And shall it in more shame be further spoken,

---

163 murtherous subornation: *secret prompting to murder*
168 line: *rank*   predicament: *situation, classification*
169 range: *stand*   173 gage them: *pledge themselves*
176 canker: *dog-rose*

Act I, Scene 3

That you are fool'd, discarded, and shook off
By him, for whom these shames ye underwent?
No. Yet time serves wherein you may redeem   180
Your banish'd honors and restore yourselves
Into the good thoughts of the world again.
Revenge the jeering and disdain'd contempt
Of this proud king, who studies day and night   184
To answer all the debt he owes to you,
Even with the bloody payment of your deaths.
Therefore I say—
   Wor.   Peace cousin, say no more.
And now I will unclasp a secret book,   188
And to your quick-conceiving discontents
I'll read you matter deep and dangerous,
As full of peril and adventurous spirit
As to o'er-walk a current roaring loud   192
On the unsteadfast footing of a spear.
   Hot. If he fall in, good night. Or sink, or swim!
Send danger from the east unto the west,
So honor cross it, from the north to south,   196
And let them grapple! O the blood more stirs
To rouse a lion than to start a hare.
   North. Imagination of some great exploit
Drives him beyond the bounds of patience.   200
   Hot. By heaven methinks it were an easy leap
To pluck bright honor from the pale-fac'd moon,
Or dive into the bottom of the deep,
Where fadom-line could never touch the ground,   204

---

183 disdain'd: *disdainful*
194 good night: *so be it*   Or . . . swim: *let him take his chance, either to sink or swim*
204 fadom-line: *sounding-rope, measured in fathoms*

34 The First Part of Henry the Fourth

And pluck up drowned honor by the locks,
So he that doth redeem her thence might wear
Without corrival all her dignities.
But out upon this half-fac'd fellowship! 208

  Wor. He apprehends a world of figures here,
But not the form of what he should attend.
Good cousin, give me audience for a while.

  Hot. I cry you mercy.

  Wor.   Those same noble Scots 212
That are your prisoners—

  Hot.   I'll keep them all!
By God he shall not have a Scot of them,
No, if a Scot would save his soul he shall not.
I'll keep them, by this hand.

  Wor.   You start away, 216
And lend no ear unto my purposes.
Those prisoners you shall keep.

  Hot.   Nay, I will; that's flat!
He said he would not ransom Mortimer,
Forbade my tongue to speak of Mortimer. 220
But I will find him when he lies asleep,
And in his ear I'll holla 'Mortimer!'
Nay,
I'll have a starling shall be taught to speak 224
Nothing but 'Mortimer,' and give it him
To keep his anger still in motion.

  Wor. Hear you, cousin; a word.

206 So: *provided that*
207 corrival: *partner*
208 half-fac'd: *one-sided*
209 apprehends: *imagines*   figures: *unpractical fancies*
212 cry you mercy: *beg your pardon*
224 starling: *a bird with remarkable powers of mimicry*

Act I, Scene 3   35

Hot. All studies here I solemnly defy,   228
Save how to gall and pinch this Bolingbroke.
And that same sword-and-buckler Prince of Wales,
But that I think his father loves him not,
And would be glad he met with some mischance,   232
I would have him poison'd with a pot of ale.

Wor. Farewell, kinsman. I will talk to you
When you are better temper'd to attend.

North. Why, what a wasp-stung and impatient fool
Art thou, to break into this woman's mood,   237
Tying thine ear to no tongue but thine own!

Hot. Why, look you, I am whipp'd and scourg'd with rods,
Nettled, and stung with pismires, when I hear   240
Of this vile politician Bolingbroke.
In Richard's time—what do you call the place?—
A plague upon't, it is in Gloucestershire—
'Twas where the madcap duke his uncle kept,   244
His uncle York—where I first bow'd my knee
Unto this king of smiles, this Bolingbroke—
'Sblood!
When you and he came back from Ravenspurgh.   248

North. At Berkeley Castle.

Hot.   You say true.
Why, what a candy deal of courtesy
This fawning greyhound then did proffer me:
'Look when his infant fortune came to age,'   252
And 'gentle Harry Percy,' and 'kind cousin.'

228 defy: *renounce*
230 sword-and-buckler: *swashbuckler, ruffianly*
240 pismires: *ants*   244 kept: *stayed*
245 York; *cf. n.*   250 candy deal: *sugary lot*
252 Look when: *whenever; cf. n.*

36   The First Part of Henry the Fourth

O, the devil take such cozeners. God forgive me!
Good uncle, tell your tale, I have done.
  Wor. Nay, if you have not, to it again.   256
We'll stay your leisure.
  Hot.   I have done, i' faith.
  Wor. Then once more to your Scottish prisoners.
Deliver them up without their ransom straight,
And make the Douglas' son your only mean   260
For powers in Scotland, which for divers reasons
Which I shall send you written, be assur'd
Will easily be granted. [*To Northumberland.*] You, my lord,
Your son in Scotland being thus employ'd,   264
Shall secretly into the bosom creep
Of that same noble prelate wellbelov'd,
The Archbishop.
  Hot. Of York, is it not?
  Wor.   True; who bears hard   268
His brother's death at Bristow, the Lord Scroop.
I speak not this in estimation,
As what I think might be, but what I know
Is ruminated, plotted, and set down,   272
And only stays but to behold the face
Of that occasion that shall bring it on.
  Hot. I smell 't! Upon my life it will do well!
  North. Before the game's afoot thou still lett'st slip.
  Hot. Why, it cannot choose but be a noble plot!   277

254 cozeners: *swindlers*
257 stay: *await*
269 Bristow: *Bristol*   Scroop; *cf. n.*
270 estimation: *conjecture*
276 still: *always*   lett'st slip: *art letting the hounds loose from the leash*

Act I, Scene 3

And then the power of Scotland, and of York,
To join with Mortimer, ha?
   Wor.   And so they shall.
   Hot. In faith, it is exceedingly well aim'd.   280
   Wor. And 'tis no little reason bids us speed,
To save our heads by raising of a head.
For bear ourselves as even as we can,
The king will always think him in our debt,   284
And think we think ourselves unsatisfied,
Till he hath found a time to pay us home.
And see already how he doth begin
To make us strangers to his looks of love.   288
   Hot. He does, he does! We'll be reveng'd on him.
   Wor. Cousin, farewell. No further go in this,
Than I by letters shall direct your course
When time is ripe, which will be suddenly.   292
I'll steal to Glendower and Lord Mortimer,
Where you and Douglas, and our powers at once,
As I will fashion it, shall happily meet,
To bear our fortunes in our own strong arms,   296
Which now we hold at much uncertainty.
   North. Farewell, good brother. We shall thrive, I trust.
   Hot. Uncle, adieu. O let the hours be short,
Till fields, and blows, and groans, applaud our sport!   300
                                          Exeunt.

---

282 head: *army*   283 even: *prudently*
290 Cousin: *kinsman*   292 suddenly: *very soon*
295 happily: *perchance, if all goes well*

ACT SECOND

SCENE FIRST

[*Rochester. The Yard of a Carriers' Inn*]

Enter a Carrier with a lantern in his hand.

1. Car. Heigh-ho! An it be not four by the day I'll be hanged. Charles' Wain is over the new chimney, and yet our horse not packed. What, ostler!

Ost. [*within*]. Anon, anon. 4

1. Car. I prithee, Tom, beat Cut's saddle, put a few flocks in the point. Poor jade is wrung in the withers, out of all cess.

Enter another Carrier.

2. Car. Peas and beans are as dank here as a dog, and that is the next way to give poor jades the bots. This house is turned upside down since Robin Ostler died. 11

1. Car. Poor fellow never joyed since the price of oats rose. It was the death of him.

Scene First. S. d.; *cf. n.*   2 Charles' Wain; *cf. n.*
5 Cut: *slang name for a horse with a docked tail*
6 flocks: *tufts of wool*   point: *head of the saddle*   wrung: *galled*
7 withers: *neck*   out of all cess: *beyond all reckoning*
8 dank: *moldy*
9 next: *most direct, surest*   bots: *disease of horses caused by worms*

Act II, Scene 1

2. Car. I think this be the most villainous house in all London road for fleas. I am stung like a tench. 15

1. Car. Like a tench! by the mass there is ne'er a king christen could be better bit than I have been since the first cock.

2. Car. Why, they will allow us ne'er a jordan, and then we leak in your chimney, and your chamber-lie breeds fleas like a loach. 21

1. Car. What, ostler, come away and be hanged, come away!

2. Car. I have a gammon of bacon, and two razes of ginger, to be delivered as far as Charing Cross. 25

1. Car. Godsbody! the turkeys in my pannier are quite starved. What, ostler? A plague on thee, hast thou never an eye in thy head? canst not hear? An 'twere not as good deed as drink to break the pate on thee, I am a very villain. Come and be hanged! hast no faith in thee? 31

Enter Gadshill.

Gads. Good morrow carriers. What's o'clock? 32

1. Car. I think it be two o'clock.

Gads. I prithee lend me thy lantern, to see my gelding in the stable.

1. Car. Nay, by God, soft! I know a trick worth two of that, i' faith. 37

---

15 tench; *cf. n.*   17 king christen: *Christian king*
19 jordan: *chamber-pot*   20 your . . . your: *colloquialism for 'any'*   chamber-lie: *urine*
21 loach: *a fish that breeds several times a year*
24 razes: *roots*   25 Charing Cross; *cf. n.*
27 starved: *perishing of cold, probably*
33 two o'clock; *cf. n.*

Gads. I pray thee lend me thine.

2. Car. Ay, when, canst tell? Lend me thy lantern, quoth he! Marry I'll see thee hanged first.

Gads. Sirrah carrier, what time do you mean to come to London?

2. Car. Time enough to go to bed with a candle, I warrant thee. Come neighbor Mugs, we'll call up the gentlemen. They will along with company, for they have great charge. *Exeunt [Carriers].*

Enter Chamberlain.

Gads. What ho, chamberlain?

Cham. 'At hand, quoth pickpurse.'

Gads. That's even as fair as 'at hand, quoth the chamberlain.' For thou variest no more from picking of purses, than giving direction doth from laboring. Thou layest the plot how.

Cham. Good morrow, Master Gadshill. It holds current that I told you yesternight. There's a franklin in the wild of Kent hath brought three hundred marks with him in gold. I heard him tell it to one of his company last night at supper—a kind of auditor, one that hath abundance of charge too, God knows what. They are up already, and call for eggs and butter. They will away presently.

Gads. Sirrah, if they meet not with Saint Nicholas' clerks, I'll give thee this neck.

---

46 charge: *baggage*
47 chamberlain: *servant in charge of guests' rooms*
53, 54 holds current: *proves true*   54 franklin: *freeholder*
55 wild: *'Weald,' an agricultural section, once wooded*
56 mark: *13s. 4d., two-thirds of a pound sterling*
61, 62 St. Nicholas' clerks: *thieves; cf. n.*

Act II, Scene 1

Cham. No, I'll none of it. I pray thee keep that for the hangman, for I know thou worshippest Saint Nicholas as truly as a man of falsehood may.

Gads. What talkest thou to me of the hangman? If I hang, I'll make a fat pair of gallows. For if I hang, old Sir John hangs with me, and thou knowest he is no starveling. Tut, there are other Trojans that thou dream'st not of, the which for sport sake are content to do the profession some grace, that would (if matters should be looked into) for their own credit sake make all whole. I am joined with no foot land-rakers, no long-staff sixpenny strikers, none of these mad mustachio-purple-hued malt worms, but with nobility, and tranquillity, burgomasters and great oneyers, such as can hold in, such as will strike sooner than speak, and speak sooner than drink, and drink sooner than pray. And yet, zounds, I lie, for they pray continually to their saint the commonwealth; or rather not pray to her, but prey on her, for they ride up and down on her, and make her their boots.

Cham. What, the commonwealth their boots? will she hold out water in foul way?

Gads. She will, she will, justice hath liquored her. We steal as in a castle, cock-sure. We have the receipt of fernseed, we walk invisible.

Cham. Nay by my faith, I think you are more beholding to the night than to fernseed for your walking invisible.

---

69 Trojans: *a cant name for rioters*
73 foot land-rakers, etc.; *cf. n.* 82 boots: *booty*
85 liquored; *cf. n.* 86 as in a castle: *in perfect security*
86, 87 receipt of fernseed; *cf. n.* 88 beholding: *obliged*

Gads. Give me thy hand. Thou shalt have a share in our purchase, as I am a true man. 92

Cham. Nay, rather let me have it, as you are a false thief.

Gads. Go to, *homo* is a common name to all men. Bid the ostler bring my gelding out of the stable. Farewell, you muddy knave. 97

Exeunt.

SCENE SECOND

[*Gadshill. On the London-Canterbury Road*]

Enter Prince, Poins, and Peto, &c.

Poins. Come, shelter, shelter! I have removed Falstaff's horse, and he frets like a gummed velvet.
Prince. Stand close.

Enter Falstaff.

Fal. Poins! Poins, and be hanged! Poins! 4
Prince. Peace, ye fat-kidneyed rascal! What a brawling dost thou keep!
Fal. Where's Poins, Hal?
Prince. He is walked up to the top of the hill. I'll go seek him. [*Withdraws.*]
Fal. I am accursed to rob in that thief's company. The rascal hath removed my horse, and tied him I know not where. If I travel but four foot by the squire further afoot, I shall break my wind. Well, I

92 purchase: *plunder* 95 *homo*; *cf. n.*   2 gummed velvet; *cf. n.*   3 close: *out of sight*
13 squire: *foot-rule*

Act II, Scene 2

doubt not but to die a fair death for all this, if I 'scape hanging for killing that rogue. I have forsworn his company hourly any time this two and twenty years, and yet I am bewitched with the rogue's company. If the rascal have not given me medicines to make me love him, I'll be hanged. It could not be else. I have drunk medicines. Poins! Hal! a plague upon you both! Bardolph! Peto! I'll starve ere I'll rob a foot further. An 'twere not as good a deed as drink to turn true man, and to leave these rogues, I am the veriest varlet that ever chewed with a tooth. Eight yards of uneven ground is threescore and ten miles afoot with me, and the stony-hearted villains know it well enough. A plague upon it when thieves can not be true one to another! 28

They whistle.

Whew! A plague upon you all! Give me my horse, you rogues! give me my horse and be hanged.

Prince [*coming forward*]. Peace, ye fatguts! Lie down, lay thine ear close to the ground, and list if thou canst hear the tread of travellers. 33

Fal. Have you any levers to lift me up again being down? 'Sblood! I'll not bear mine own flesh so far afoot again for all the coin in thy father's exchequer. What a plague mean ye to colt me thus? 37

Prince. Thou liest. Thou art not colted, thou art uncolted.

Fal. I prithee, good Prince, Hal, help me to my horse, good king's son. 41

Prince. Out, ye rogue! shall I be your ostler?

---

19 medicines: *love potions* (cf. *Othello I. iii. 61*)
37 colt: *make a fool of*

44   The First Part of Henry the Fourth

Fal. Hang thyself in thine own heir-apparent garters! If I be ta'en, I'll peach for this. An I have not ballads made on you all, and sung to filthy tunes, let a cup of sack be my poison. When a jest is so forward, and afoot too, I hate it.   47

Enter Gadshill [and Bardolph].

Gads. Stand.

Fal. So I do, against my will.

Poins. O 'tis our setter. I know his voice. Bardolph, what news?   51

Bard. Case ye, case ye! on with your vizards! There's money of the king's coming down the hill. 'Tis going to the king's exchequer.

Fal. You lie, ye rogue, 'tis going to the king's tavern.   56

Gads. There's enough to make us all.

Fal. To be hanged.

Prince. Sirs, you four shall front them in the narrow lane. Ned Poins and I will walk lower. If they 'scape from your encounter, then they light on us.   61

Peto. How many be there of them?

Gads. Some eight or ten.   63

Fal. 'Zounds! will they not rob us?

Prince. What, a coward, Sir John Paunch?

Fal. Indeed I am not John of Gaunt your grandfather, but yet no coward, Hal.   67

Prince. Well, we leave that to the proof.

43 heir-apparent garters; *cf. n.*   44 peach: *turn informer*
47 forward: *bold*
50 setter: *the one who set the match; cf. I. ii. 109*
52 Case ye: *put on your masks*
66 John of Gaunt; *cf. n.*   68 proof: *test*

Act II, Scene 2

Poins. Sirrah Jack, thy horse stands behind the hedge. When thou needst him, there thou shalt find him. Farewell, and stand fast. 71

Fal. Now can not I strike him if I should be hanged.

Prince. Ned, where are our disguises?

Poins. Here, hard by. Stand close. 75

[*Prince and Poins withdraw.*]

Fal. Now my masters, happy man be his dole, say I. Every man to his business.

Enter the Travellers.

Trav. Come, neighbor, the boy shall lead our horses down the hill. We'll walk afoot awhile and ease our legs. 80

Thieves. Stand!

Trav. Jesus bless us!

Fal. Strike! down with them! cut the villains' throats! Ah, whoreson caterpillars, bacon-fed knaves, they hate us youth. Down with them! fleece them!

Trav. O we are undone, both we and ours for ever! 87

Fal. Hang ye, gorbellied knaves, are ye undone? No, ye fat chuffs, I would your store were here! On, bacons, on! What, ye knaves, young men must live. You are grand-jurors, are ye? We'll jure ye, i' faith. 91

Here they rob them and bind them. Exeunt.
Enter the Prince and Poins.

76 happy man be his dole: *happiness be his portion, or, luck be with us*
84 whoreson: *miserable*
88 gorbellied: *fat-paunched*   89 chuffs: *misers*
90 bacons: *rustics*   91 jure: *a verb of Falstaff's own making*

Prince. The thieves have bound the true men. Now could thou and I rob the thieves, and go merrily to London, it would be argument for a week, laughter for a month, and a good jest for ever. 95

Poins. Stand close. I hear them coming.

Enter the thieves again.

Fal. Come my masters, let us share, and then to horse before day. An the Prince and Poins be not two arrant cowards there's no equity stirring. There's no more valor in that Poins, than in a wild duck. 100

Prince. Your money!

Poins. Villains!

As they are sharing, the Prince and Poins set upon them. They all run away, and Falstaff after a blow or two runs away too, leaving the booty behind them.

Prince. Got with much ease. Now merrily to horse. The thieves are all scatter'd, and possess'd with fear 104
So strongly, that they dare not meet each other.
Each takes his fellow for an officer.
Away, good Ned. Falstaff sweats to death
And lards the lean earth as he walks along. 108
Were't not for laughing I should pity him.

Poins. How the fat rogue roar'd! *Exeunt.*

94 argument: *subject for conversation*
99 no equity stirring: *no such thing as fair judgment*

Act II, Scene 3

SCENE THIRD

[*Warkworth Castle, Northumberland*]

Enter Hotspur, solus, reading a letter.

But for mine own part, my lord, I could be well contented to be there, in respect of the love I bear your house.

He could be contented! Why is he not then? In the respect of the love he bears our house! He shows in this, he loves his own barn better than he loves our house. Let me see some more. 6

The purpose you undertake is dangerous—

Why, that's certain. 'Tis dangerous to take a cold, to sleep, to drink. But I tell you, my lord fool, out of this nettle danger, we pluck this flower safety. 10

The purpose you undertake is dangerous, the friends you have named uncertain, the time itself unsorted, and your whole plot too light, for the counterpoise of so great an opposition.

Say you so? say you so? I say unto you again, you are a shallow cowardly hind, and you lie. What a lack-brain is this! By the Lord our plot is a good plot as ever was laid, our friends true and constant! a good plot, good friends, and full of expectation! an excellent plot, very good friends! What a frosty-spirited rogue is this! Why, my lord of York commends the plot, and the general course of the action.

Scene Third. S. d.; *cf. n.*
12 unsorted: *ill-chosen*   16 hind: *servant, slave*

48   The First Part of Henry the Fourth

'Zounds! an I were now by this rascal I could brain him with his lady's fan. Is there not my father, my uncle, and myself? Lord Edmund Mortimer, my lord of York, and Owen Glendower? Is there not besides the Douglas? Have I not all their letters to meet me in arms by the ninth of the next month, and are they not some of them set forward already? What a pagan rascal is this, an infidel! Ha! You shall see now in very sincerity of fear and cold heart will he to the king and lay open all our proceedings. O, I could divide myself, and go to buffets, for moving such a dish of skim milk with so honorable an action. Hang him, let him tell the king! We are prepared. I will set forward to-night.   36

Enter his Lady.

How now, Kate! I must leave you within these two hours.
  Lady P. O my good lord, why are you thus alone?
For what offence have I this fortnight been
A banish'd woman from my Harry's bed?   40
Tell me sweet lord, what is't that takes from thee
Thy stomach, pleasure, and thy golden sleep?
Why dost thou bend thine eyes upon the earth,
And start so often when thou sitt'st alone?   44
Why hast thou lost the fresh blood in thy cheeks,
And given my treasures and my rights of thee
To thick-eyed musing, and curst melancholy?
In thy faint slumbers I by thee have watch'd,   48
And heard thee murmur tales of iron wars,

33 divide myself; *cf. n.*
37 Kate; *cf. n.*
46, 47 *Cf. n.*
42 stomach: *appetite*
47 curst: *perverse*

Act II, Scene 3

Speak terms of manage to thy bounding steed,
Cry 'Courage! to the field!' And thou hast talk'd
Of sallies and retires, of trenches, tents, 52
Of palisadoes, frontiers, parapets,
Of basilisks, of cannon, culverin,
Of prisoners' ransom, and of soldiers slain,
And all the currents of a heady fight. 56
Thy spirit within thee hath been so at war,
And thus hath so bestirr'd thee in thy sleep,
That beads of sweat have stood upon thy brow
Like bubbles in a late-disturbed stream; 60
And in thy face strange motions have appear'd,
Such as we see when men restrain their breath,
On some great sudden hest. O what portents are these?
Some heavy business hath my lord in hand, 64
And I must know it. Else he loves me not.

Hot. What ho! [*Enter Servant.*] Is Gilliams with the packet gone?

Serv. He is, my lord, an hour ago.

Hot. Hath Butler brought those horses from the sheriff? 68

Serv. One horse, my lord, he brought even now.

Hot. What horse? a roan? a crop-ear is it not?

Serv. It is, my lord.

Hot.   That roan shall be my throne.
Well, I will back him straight. O, *Esperance!* 72

---

50 manage: *direction*   52 retires: *retreats*
53 palisadoes: *sharp stakes driven into the ground as defence against cavalry*   frontiers: *outworks; cf. I. iii. 19*
54 basilisks; *cf. n.*
56 currents: *drifts, movements*   heady: *headlong*
63 hest: *command*
72 Esperance: *the motto of the Percy family*

50   The First Part of Henry the Fourth

Bid Butler lead him forth into the park.

[*Exit Servant.*]

   Lady P. But hear you, my lord.
   Hot. What sayst thou, my lady?
   Lady P. What is it carries you away?
   Hot. Why, my horse (my love), my horse.
   Lady P. Out, you mad-headed ape!
A weasel hath not such a deal of spleen
As you are toss'd with. In faith
I'll know your business, Harry, that I will.
I fear my brother Mortimer doth stir,
About his title, and hath sent for you
To line his enterprise. But if you go—
   Hot. So far afoot, I shall be weary, love.
   Lady P. Come, come, you paraquito! answer me
Directly unto this question that I ask.
In faith I'll break thy little finger, Harry,
An if thou wilt not tell me all things true.
   Hot. Away,
Away, you trifler! Love, I love thee not.
I care not for thee, Kate. This is no world
To play with mammets and to tilt with lips.
We must have bloody noses, and crack'd crowns,
And pass them current too. God's me, my horse!
What sayst thou, Kate? what wouldst thou have with me?
   Lady P. Do you not love me? do you not indeed?
Well, do not then, for since you love me not
I will not love myself. Do you not love me?
Nay, tell me if you speak in jest or no.

79 spleen: *caprice*
93 mammets: *dolls*
84 line: *strengthen*
94 crack'd crowns; *cf. n.*

Act II, Scene 3   51

Hot. Come, wilt thou see me ride?
And when I am o' horseback I will swear
I love thee infinitely. But hark you Kate,
I must not have you henceforth question me   104
Whither I go, nor reason whereabout.
Whither I must, I must. And to conclude,
This evening must I leave you, gentle Kate.
I know you wise, but yet no farther wise   108
Than Harry Percy's wife. Constant you are,
But yet a woman; and for secrecy
No lady closer, for I well believe
Thou wilt not utter what thou dost not know,   112
And so far will I trust thee, gentle Kate.
  Lady P. How! so far?
  Hot. Not an inch further. But hark you Kate;
Whither I go, thither shall you go too.   116
To-day will I set forth, to-morrow you.
Will this content you, Kate?
  Lady P.   It must, of force.   *Exeunt.*

SCENE FOURTH

[*The Boar's Head Tavern, Eastcheap, London*]

Enter Prince and Poins.

  Prince. Ned, prithee come out of that fat room,
and lend me thy hand to laugh a little.
  Poins. Where hast been, Hal?   3
  Prince. With three or four loggerheads, amongst

---

1 fat: *close, stuffy; cf. n.*

three or four score hogsheads. I have sounded the
very bass-string of humility. Sirrah, I am sworn
brother to a leash of drawers, and can call them all
by their christen names, as Tom, Dick, and Francis.
They take it already upon their salvation, that
though I be but Prince of Wales, yet I am the king
of courtesy, and tell me flatly I am no proud Jack
like Falstaff, but a Corinthian, a lad of mettle, a
good boy (by the Lord so they call me), and when I
am King of England I shall command all the good
lads in Eastcheap. They call drinking deep 'dyeing
scarlet,' and when you breathe in your watering they
cry 'hem!' and bid you play it off. To conclude, I am
so good a proficient in one quarter of an hour that
I can drink with any tinker in his own language,
during my life. I tell thee, Ned, thou hast lost much
honor, that thou wert not with me in this action. But
sweet Ned—to sweeten which name of Ned, I give
thee this pennyworth of sugar, clapped even now into
my hand by an underskinker, one that never spake
other English in his life than 'Eight shillings and sixpence,' and 'You are welcome,' with this shrill addition, 'Anon, anon, sir!' 'Score a pint of bastard in the
Half-moon,' or so. But Ned, to drive away the time
till Falstaff come, I prithee do thou stand in some
by-room, while I question my puny drawer to what

---

7 leash: *three on a string*   drawers: *waiters*
9 take it . . . upon: *swear by*   12 Corinthian: *gay fellow*
16 breathe . . . watering: *stop to breathe while drinking*
17 play: *toss*   19 tinker; *cf. n.*
24 underskinker: *under-tapster*
27 bastard: *sweet Spanish wine*
28 Half-moon: *name of a room in the inn*

Act II, Scene 4   53

end he gave me the sugar, and do thou never leave calling 'Francis!' that his tale to me may be nothing but 'Anon.' Step aside and I'll show thee a precedent.   34

Poins. Francis!

Prince. Thou art perfect.— [*Exit Poins.*] Francis!

Enter Drawer [*Francis*].

Fran. Anon, anon, sir. Look down into the Pomgarnet, Ralph.

Prince. Come hither, Francis.   40

Fran. My lord.

Prince. How long hast thou to serve, Francis?

Fran. Forsooth, five years, and as much as to—

Poins [*within*]. Francis!   44

Fran. Anon, anon, sir.

Prince. Five years! by'r lady a long lease for the clinking of pewter; but Francis, darest thou be so valiant, as to play the coward with thy indenture, and show it a fair pair of heels, and run from it?   49

Fran. O Lord, sir! I'll be sworn upon all the books in England, I could find in my heart—

Poins [*within*]. Francis!   52

Fran. Anon, sir.

Prince. How old art thou, Francis?

Fran. Let me see—about Michaelmas next I shall be—   56

Poins [*within*]. Francis!

33 precedent: *example*
38 Pomgarnet: *'Pomegranate,' a room in the inn*
42 to serve: *i.e., as apprentice to the Vintner*
48 indenture: *contract*   55 Michaelmas; *cf. n.*

Fran. Anon, sir. Pray stay a little, my lord.

Prince. Nay but hark you, Francis. For the sugar thou gavest me—'twas a pennyworth, was't not? 60

Fran. O Lord, I would it had been two.

Prince. I will give thee for it a thousand pound. Ask me when thou wilt, and thou shalt have it.

Poins [*within*]. Francis! 64

Fran. Anon, anon.

Prince. Anon, Francis? No, Francis, but tomorrow, Francis. Or, Francis, o' Thursday. Or indeed, Francis, when thou wilt. But Francis! 68

Fran. My lord?

Prince. Wilt thou rob this leathern-jerkin, crystal-button, not-pated, agate-ring, puke-stocking, caddis-garter, smooth-tongue, Spanish-pouch— 72

Fran. O Lord sir, who do you mean?

Prince. Why then, your brown bastard is your only drink. For look you, Francis, your white canvas doublet will sully. In Barbary, sir, it cannot come to so much. 77

Fran. What, sir?

Poins [*within*]. Francis!

Prince. Away, you rogue! Dost thou not hear them call? 81

> *Here they both call him. The Drawer stands amazed, not knowing which way to go.*
>
> *Enter Vintner.*

Vint. What! stand'st thou still, and hear'st such a calling? Look to the guests within. [*Exit Francis.*]

---

71 not-pated: *nut-pated, with closely cropped head* puke: *dark-colored and woolen* caddis: *cheap yarn*
74ff.; *cf. n.*

Act II, Scene 4   55

My lord, old Sir John with half a dozen more are
at the door. Shall I let them in?   85

Prince. Let them alone awhile, and then open the
door. [*Exit Vintner.*] Poins!

Poins [*within*]. Anon, anon, sir.   88

Enter Poins.

Prince. Sirrah, Falstaff and the rest of the thieves
are at the door. Shall we be merry?

Poins. As merry as crickets, my lad. But hark ye,
what cunning match have you made with this jest of
the drawer? Come, what's the issue?   93

Prince. I am now of all humors, that have showed
themselves humors since the old days of goodman
Adam to the pupil age of this present twelve o'clock
at midnight. [*Francis crosses the stage.*] What's
o'clock, Francis?   98

Fran. Anon, anon, sir.   [*Exit.*]

Prince. That ever this fellow should have fewer
words than a parrot, and yet the son of a woman!
His industry is up-stairs and down-stairs, his elo-
quence the parcel of a reckoning. I am not yet of
Percy's mind, the Hotspur of the North, he that kills
me some six or seven dozen of Scots at a breakfast,
washes his hands, and says to his wife, 'Fie upon this
quiet life! I want work.' 'O my sweet Harry,' says
she, 'how many hast thou killed to-day?' 'Give my
roan horse a drench,' says he, and answers, 'Some
fourteen,' an hour after, 'a trifle, a trifle.' I prithee

92 match: *game*   96 pupil age: *mere child's age*
103 parcel of a reckoning: *an item on a bill*
103, 104 not yet of Percy's mind; *cf. n.*
109 drench: *bran and water*

call in Falstaff. I'll play Percy, and that damned brawn shall play Dame Mortimer his wife. 'Rivo!' says the drunkard. Call in Ribs, call in Tallow. 113

Enter Falstaff, [Bardolph, Peto, and Gadshill. The Drawer follows with wine].

Poins. Welcome, Jack! Where hast thou been?

Fal. A plague of all cowards I say, and a vengeance too! marry and amen! Give me a cup of sack, boy. Ere I lead this life long I'll sew nether-stocks and mend them, and foot them too. A plague of all cowards! Give me a cup of sack, rogue.—Is there no virtue extant? *He drinketh.*

Prince. Didst thou never see Titan kiss a dish of butter—pitiful-hearted Titan—that melted at the sweet tale of the sun's? If thou didst, then behold that compound. 124

Fal. You rogue, here's lime in this sack too. There is nothing but roguery to be found in villainous man. Yet a coward is worse than a cup of sack with lime in it, a villainous coward! Go thy ways, old Jack; die when thou wilt. If manhood, good manhood, be not forgot upon the face of the earth, then am I a shotten herring. There lives not three good men unhanged in England, and one of them is fat, and grows old. God help the while! a bad world I say. I would I were a weaver. I could sing psalms, or anything. A plague of all cowards I say still. 135

112 brawn: *fattened pig*   'Rivo': *a Spanish (?) exclamation of drunkards*
117 nether-stocks: *stockings*   120 virtue: *courage*
121 Titan, etc.; *cf. n.*   123 sweet . . . sun's; *cf. n.*
131 shotten herring: *a herring that has cast its roe*
134 weaver; *cf. n.*

Act II, Scene 4

Prince. How now wool-sack! what mutter you?

Fal. A king's son! If I do not beat thee out of thy kingdom with a dagger of lath, and drive all thy subjects afore thee like a flock of wild geese, I'll never wear hair on my face more. You Prince of Wales! 141

Prince. Why you whoreson round man, what's the matter?

Fal. Are not you a coward? Answer me to that. And Poins there? 145

Poins. 'Zounds ye fat paunch, an ye call me coward, by the Lord I'll stab thee.

Fal. I call thee coward? I'll see thee damned ere I call thee coward, but I would give a thousand pound I could run as fast as thou canst. You are straight enough in the shoulders, you care not who sees your back. Call you that backing of your friends? A plague upon such backing! give me them that will face me. Give me a cup of sack. I am a rogue if I drunk to-day. 155

Prince. O villain! thy lips are scarce wiped since thou drunk'st last.

Fal. All is one for that. A plague of all cowards, still say I. *He drinketh.*

Prince. What's the matter? 160

Fal. What's the matter? there be four of us here have ta'en a thousand pound this day morning.

Prince. Where is it, Jack? where is it?

Fal. Where is it? Taken from us it is. A hundred upon poor four of us. 165

Prince. What, a hundred, man?

Fal. I am a rogue if I were not at half-sword with

167 at half-sword: *at close quarters*

58 The First Part of Henry the Fourth

a dozen of them two hours together. I have 'scap'd by miracle. I am eight times thrust through the doublet, four through the hose, my buckler cut through and through, my sword hacked like a handsaw: *ecce signum!* I never dealt better since I was a man. All would not do. A plague of all cowards! Let them speak. If they speak more or less than truth, they are villains, and the sons of darkness. 175

Prince. Speak, sirs. How was it?

Gads. We four set upon some dozen—

Fal. Sixteen at least, my lord.

Gads. And bound them.

Peto. No, no, they were not bound. 180

Fal. You rogue, they were bound, every man of them, or I am a Jew else, an Ebrew Jew.

Gads. As we were sharing, some six or seven fresh men set upon us— 184

Fal. And unbound the rest, and then come in the other.

Prince. What, fought you with them all?

Fal. All? I know not what you call all, but if I fought not with fifty of them I am a bunch of radish. If there were not two or three and fifty upon poor old Jack, then am I no two-legg'd creature. 191

Prince. Pray God you have not murdered some of them.

Fal. Nay, that's past praying for. I have peppered two of them. Two I am sure I have paid, two rogues in buckram suits. I tell thee what, Hal, if I tell thee a lie, spit in my face, call me horse. Thou knowest my

171 *ecce signum: behold the proof*
186 other: *others*
176–184 Cf. *n.*
195 paid: *killed*

Act II, Scene 4

old ward. Here I lay, and thus I bore my point. Four rogues in buckram let drive at me—

Prince. What, four? Thou saidst but two even now. 201

Fal. Four, Hal. I told thee four.

Poins. Ay, ay, he said four.

Fal. These four came all a-front, and mainly thrust at me. I made me no more ado, but took all their seven points in my target, thus. 206

Prince. Seven? Why, there were but four even now.

Fal. In buckram?

Poins. Ay, four in buckram suits.

Fal. Seven, by these hilts, or I am a villain else.

Prince. Prithee let him alone. We shall have more anon. 213

Fal. Dost thou hear me, Hal?

Prince. Ay, and mark thee too, Jack.

Fal. Do so, for it is worth the listening to. These nine in buckram that I told thee of— 217

Prince. So, two more already.

Fal. Their points being broken—

Poins. Down fell their hose.

Fal. Began to give me ground. But I followed me close, came in, foot and hand, and with a thought, seven of the eleven I paid.

Prince. O monstrous! Eleven buckram men grown out of two. 225

Fal. But as the devil would have it, three misbe-

---

198 ward: *fencer's posture of defence*
204 mainly: *strongly (cf. might and main)*   206 target: *shield*
211 these hilts: *the cross-hilt of his sword*   219 points; *cf. n.*

gotten knaves in Kendal green came at my back, and let drive at me—for it was so dark, Hal, that thou couldst not see thy hand. 229

Prince. These lies are like their father that begets them, gross as a mountain, open, palpable. Why thou clay-brained guts, thou knotty-pated fool, thou whoreson obscene greasy tallow-catch— 233

Fal. What, art thou mad? art thou mad? Is not the truth the truth?

Prince. Why, how couldst thou know these men in Kendal green, when it was so dark thou couldst not see thy hand? Come, tell us your reason. What sayest thou to this?

Poins. Come, your reason, Jack, your reason. 240

Fal. What, upon compulsion? 'Zounds! an I were at the strappado, or all the racks in the world, I would not tell you on compulsion. Give you a reason on compulsion? If reasons were as plentiful as blackberries, I would give no man a reason upon compulsion, I.

Prince. I'll be no longer guilty of this sin. This sanguine coward, this bed-presser, this horse-back-breaker, this huge hill of flesh— 248

Fal. 'Sblood, you starveling, you elf-skin, you dried neat's-tongue, you bull's pizzle, you stockfish! O for breath to utter what is like thee, you tailor's yard, you sheath, you bowcase, you vile standing-tuck— 252

---

227 Kendal green; *cf. n.*   232 knotty-pated: *thick-headed*
233 tallow-catch: *lump of tallow (tallow-keech)* ? *tub of tallow (tallow-ketch)* ?
242 strappado; *cf. n.*
244 reasons; *cf. n.*   247 sanguine: *red-faced*
250 neat's-tongue: *ox tongue*   stockfish: *dried cod*
252 standing-tuck: *small rapier standing on end*

Act II, Scene 4

Prince. Well, breathe awhile, and then to it again, and when thou hast tired thyself in base comparisons, hear me speak but this.

Poins. Mark, Jack.

Prince. We two saw you four set on four, and [you] bound them and were masters of their wealth. Mark now how a plain tale shall put you down. Then did we two set on you four and, with a word, outfaced you from your prize, and have it, yea, and can show it you here in the house. And Falstaff, you carried your guts away as nimbly, with as quick dexterity, and roared for mercy, and still run and roared, as ever I heard bull-calf. What a slave art thou to hack thy sword as thou hast done, and then say it was in fight! What trick, what device, what starting-hole canst thou now find out, to hide thee from this open and apparent shame?

Poins. Come, let's hear, Jack. What trick hast thou now?

Fal. By the Lord, I knew ye as well as he that made ye. Why, hear you, my masters. Was it for me to kill the heir-apparent? Should I turn upon the true prince? Why, thou knowest I am as valiant as Hercules: but beware instinct, the lion will not touch the true prince. Instinct is a great matter. I was now a coward on instinct. I shall think the better of myself and thee during my life; I for a valiant lion, and thou for a true prince. But by the Lord, lads, I am glad you have the money. Hostess, clap

---

261 outfaced: *frightened*
267 starting-hole: *subterfuge (hunted animal's shelter)*
272 I knew ye; *cf. n.*

to the doors, watch to-night, pray to-morrow. Gallants, lads, boys, hearts of gold, all the titles of good fellowship come to you! What, shall we be merry? shall we have a play extempore? 285

Prince. Content. And the argument shall be thy running away.

Fal. Ah! no more of that, Hal, an thou lovest me!

Enter Hostess.

Host. O Jesu, my lord the prince!

Prince. How now my lady the hostess! what say'st thou to me? 291

Host. Marry my lord, there is a nobleman of the court at door would speak with you. He says he comes from your father.

Prince. Give him as much as will make him a royal man, and send him back again to my mother. 296

Fal. What manner of man is he?

Host. An old man.

Fal. What doth gravity out of his bed at midnight? Shall I give him his answer? 300

Prince. Prithee do, Jack.

Fal. Faith, and I'll send him packing. *Exit.*

Prince. Now sirs, by'r lady you fought fair. So did you, Peto, so did you, Bardolph. You are lions too, you ran away upon instinct, you will not touch the true prince; no, fie! 306

Bard. Faith, I ran when I saw others run.

Prince. Faith, tell me now in earnest, how came Falstaff's sword so hacked?

Peto. Why, he hacked it with his dagger, and said

295 royal; *cf. n.*

Act II, Scene 4 63

he would swear truth out of England, but he would make you believe it was done in fight, and persuaded us to do the like. 313

Bard. Yea, and to tickle our noses with speargrass, to make them bleed, and then to beslubber our garments with it, and swear it was the blood of true men. I did that I did not this seven year before, I blushed to hear his monstrous devices. 318

Prince. O villain! thou stolest a cup of sack eighteen years ago and wert taken with the manner, and ever since thou hast blushed extempore. Thou hadst fire and sword on thy side, and yet thou ranst away; what instinct hadst thou for it? 323

Bard. [*pointing to his own face*]. My lord, do you see these meteors? Do you behold these exhalations?

Prince. I do.

Bard. What think you they portend?

Prince. Hot livers, and cold purses. 328

Bard. Choler, my lord, if rightly taken.

Prince. No, if rightly taken, halter.

Enter Falstaff.

Here comes lean Jack, here comes Barebone. How now my sweet creature of bombast! How long is't ago, Jack, since thou sawest thine own knee? 332

Fal. My own knee! When I was about thy years, Hal, I was not an eagle's talon in the waist. I could have crept into any alderman's thumb-ring. A plague

320 taken . . . manner: *taken in the act*
324–330 Cf. n. 325 exhalations: *meteors*
329 rightly taken: *correctly diagnosed*
330 rightly taken: *justly arrested*
332 bombast: *cotton stuffing*

of sighing and grief! it blows a man up like a bladder. There's villainous news abroad. Here was Sir John Bracy from your father. You must to the court in the morning. That same mad fellow of the North, Percy, and he of Wales that gave Amamon the bastinado and made Lucifer cuckold, and swore the devil his true liegeman upon the cross of a Welsh hook—what a plague call you him? 344

Poins. O, Glendower.

Fal. Owen, Owen, the same; and his son-in-law Mortimer, and old Northumberland, and that sprightly Scot of Scots, Douglas, that runs a-horseback up a hill perpendicular. 349

Prince. He that rides at high speed, and with his pistol kills a sparrow flying.

Fal. You have hit it. 352

Prince. So did he never the sparrow.

Fal. Well, that rascal hath good mettle in him. He will not run.

Prince. Why, what a rascal art thou then, to praise him so for running! 357

Fal. A-horseback, ye cuckoo; but afoot he will not budge a foot.

Prince. Yes, Jack, upon instinct. 360

Fal. I grant ye, upon instinct. Well, he is there too, and one Mordake, and a thousand bluecaps more. Worcester is stolen away to-night. Thy father's beard is turned white with the news. You may buy land now as cheap as stinking mackerel. 365

---

341 Amamon: *a devil; cf. n.*   bastinado: *a cudgelling*
343 Welsh hook: *weapon resembling a halberd*
362 bluecaps: *Scots (so called from their blue bonnets)*

Act II, Scene 4   65

Prince. Why then, it is like if there come a hot June, and this civil buffeting hold, we shall buy maidenheads as they buy hobnails, by the hundreds.

Fal. By the mass, lad, thou sayest true. It is like we shall have good trading that way. But tell me, Hal, art not thou horrible afeard? Thou being heir-apparent, could the world pick thee out three such enemies again as that fiend Douglas, that spirit Percy, and that devil Glendower? Art thou not horribly afraid? doth not thy blood thrill at it?   375

Prince. Not a whit, i' faith. I lack some of thy instinct.

Fal. Well, thou wilt be horribly chid to-morrow when thou comest to thy father. If thou love me, practise an answer.   380

Prince. Do thou stand for my father and examine me upon the particulars of my life.

Fal. Shall I? Content. This chair shall be my state, this dagger my scepter, and this cushion my crown.   384

Prince. Thy state is taken for a joined-stool, thy golden scepter for a leaden dagger, and thy precious rich crown for a pitiful bald crown.

Fal. Well, an the fire of grace be not quite out of thee, now shalt thou be moved. Give me a cup of sack to make my eyes look red, that it may be thought I have wept, for I must speak in passion, and I will do it in King Cambyses' vein.   392

Prince. Well, here is my leg.

Fal. And here is my speech. Stand aside, nobility.

Host. O Jesu! This is excellent sport, i' faith!

383 state: *throne of state*   391 passion: *deep feeling*
392 Cambyses'; *cf. n.*   393 leg: *bow*

66 The First Part of Henry the Fourth

Fal. Weep not, sweet queen, for trickling tears are vain.

Host. O, the father! how he holds his countenance!

Fal. For God's sake, lords, convey my tristful queen,
For tears do stop the floodgates of her eyes.

Host. O Jesu, he doth it as like one of these harlotry players as ever I see! 401

Fal. Peace, good pintpot, peace, good tickle-brain.

[*Bardolph conveys the Hostess from the stage.*]

—Harry, I do not only marvel where thou spendest thy time, but also how thou are accompanied. For though the camomile, the more it is trodden on, the faster it grows, yet youth, the more it is wasted, the sooner it wears. That thou art my son, I have partly thy mother's word, partly my own opinion, but chiefly a villainous trick of thine eye, and a foolish hanging of thy nether lip, that doth warrant me. If then thou be son to me, here lies the point: why, being son to me, art thou so pointed at? Shall the blessed sun of heaven prove a micher, and eat blackberries? A question not to be asked. Shall the son of England prove a thief, and take purses? A question to be asked. There is a thing, Harry, which thou hast often heard of, and it is known to many in our land by the name of pitch. This pitch (as ancient writers do report) doth defile; so doth the company thou keepest. For, Harry, now I do not speak to thee in drink, but in tears; not in pleasure, but in passion; not in words only, but in woes also. And yet there is

397 the father: *i.e., Falstaff in the role of father*
398 tristful: *sorrowful*   400 harlotry: *rascally*
402 tickle-brain: *a strong liquor; cf. n.*
403ff.; *Cf. n.*   405 camomile: *a strong-scented herb*
410 nether: *lower*   413 micher: *truant*

Act II, Scene 4

a virtuous man, whom I have often noted in thy company, but I know not his name. 424

Prince. What manner of man, an it like your Majesty?

Fal. A goodly portly man, i' faith, and a corpulent; of a cheerful look, a pleasing eye, and a most noble carriage; and as I think, his age some fifty, or by'r lady inclining to threescore. And now I remember me, his name is Falstaff. If that man should be lewdly given, he deceiveth me. For, Harry, I see virtue in his looks. If then the tree may be known by the fruit, as the fruit by the tree, then peremptorily I speak it, there is virtue in that Falstaff. Him keep with, the rest banish. And tell me now thou naughty varlet, tell me where hast thou been this month?

Prince. Dost thou speak like a king? Do thou stand for me, and I'll play my father. 439

Fal. Depose me? If thou dost it half so gravely, so majestically, both in word and matter, hang me up by the heels for a rabbit-sucker, or a poulter's hare.

Prince. Well, here I am set.

Fal. And here I stand. Judge, my masters. 444

Prince. Now Harry, whence come you?

Fal. My noble lord, from Eastcheap.

Prince. The complaints I hear of thee are grievous.

Fal. 'Sblood, my lord, they are false! [*Aside to Prince.*] Nay, I'll tickle ye for a young prince, i' faith.

Prince. Swearest thou, ungracious boy? Henceforth ne'er look on me. Thou art violently carried away from grace. There is a devil haunts thee in the

442 Cf. *n.*
449 Cf. *n.* 450, 451 Henceforth, etc.; cf. *n.*

68 The First Part of Henry the Fourth

likeness of an old fat man, a tun of man is thy companion. Why dost thou converse with that trunk of humors, that bolting-hutch of beastliness, that swoln parcel of dropsies, that huge bombard of sack, that stuffed cloak-bag of guts, that roasted Manningtree ox with the pudding in his belly, that reverend vice, that grey iniquity, that father ruffian, that vanity in years? Wherein is he good, but to taste sack and drink it? wherein neat and cleanly, but to carve a capon and eat it? wherein cunning, but in craft? wherein crafty, but in villainy? wherein villainous, but in all things? wherein worthy, but in nothing? 464

Fal. I would your Grace would take me with you. Whom means your Grace?

Prince. That villainous abominable misleader of youth, Falstaff, that old white-bearded Satan. 468

Fal. My lord, the man I know.

Prince. I know thou dost.

Fal. But to say I know more harm in him than in myself, were to say more than I know. That he is old, the more the pity, his white hairs do witness it; but that he is (saving your reverence) a whoremaster, that I utterly deny. If sack and sugar be a fault, God help the wicked! If to be old and merry be a sin, then many an old host that I know is damned.

---

454 trunk of humors: *chest full of infirmities*
455 bolting-hutch: *bin for sifting meal*
456 bombard: *large leather vessel for holding liquor*
457 cloak-bag: *portmanteau* Manningtree; *cf. n.*
465 take me with you: *let me follow your meaning*
474 saving . . . reverence: *an apologetic phrase introducing a remark that might offend the hearer*

Act II, Scene 4

If to be fat be to be hated, then Pharaoh's lean kine are to be loved. No, my good lord, banish Peto, banish Bardolph, banish Poins; but for sweet Jack Falstaff, kind Jack Falstaff, true Jack Falstaff, valiant Jack Falstaff, and therefore more valiant, being, as he is, old Jack Falstaff—banish not him thy Harry's company, banish not him thy Harry's company. Banish plump Jack, and banish all the world. 485

Prince. I do, I will.

Enter Bardolph running.

Bard. O my lord, my lord! the sheriff with a most monstrous watch is at the door. 488

Fal. Out ye rogue! Play out the play. I have much to say in the behalf of that Falstaff.

Enter the Hostess.

Host. O Jesu, my lord, my lord!

Prince. Heigh, heigh! the devil rides upon a fiddlestick. What's the matter? 493

Host. The sheriff and all the watch are at the door. They are come to search the house. Shall I let them in? 496

Fal. Dost thou hear, Hal? Never call a true piece of gold a counterfeit. Thou art essentially mad without seeming so.

Prince. And thou a natural coward without instinct. 501

Fal. I deny your major. If you will deny the sheriff,

---

478 Pharaoh's lean kine; *cf. n.*
483–485 banish not him, etc.; *cf. n.*
497–499 Cf. *n.*   502 major: *major premise; cf. n.*

70   The First Part of Henry the Fourth

so; if not, let him enter. If I become not a cart as well as another man, a plague on my bringing up! I hope I shall as soon be strangled with a halter as another.   506

  Prince. Go hide thee behind the arras. The rest walk up above. Now my masters, for a true face and good conscience.

  Fal. Both which I have had, but their date is out, and therefore I'll hide me.   *Exit.*

  Prince. Call in the sheriff.   512

Enter Sheriff and the Carrier.

Now master sheriff, what is your will with me?

  Sher. First pardon me, my lord. A hue and cry
Hath follow'd certain men unto this house.

  Prince. What men?   516

  Sher. One of them is well known, my gracious lord,
A gross fat man.

  Car.   As fat as butter.

  Prince. The man, I do assure you, is not here,
For I myself at this time have employ'd him.   520
And sheriff, I will engage my word to thee,
That I will by to-morrow dinner-time
Send him to answer thee or any man,
For anything he shall be charg'd withal.   524
And so let me entreat you leave the house.

  Sher. I will, my lord. There are two gentlemen
Have in this robbery lost three hundred marks.

---

503 cart: *cart used for taking criminals to the gallows*
507 arras: *hanging screen of tapestry placed around the walls of a room*
507, 508 *Cf. n.*   519, 520 *Cf. n.*

Act II, Scene 4

Prince. It may be so. If he have robb'd these men he shall be answerable. And so farewell.

Sher. Good night, my noble lord.

Prince. I think it is good morrow, is it not?

Sher. Indeed, my lord, I think it be two o'clock.
Exit [with Carrier].

Prince. This oily rascal is known as well as Paul's. Go call him forth.

Peto. Falstaff!—Fast asleep behind the arras, and snorting like a horse.

Prince. Hark, how hard he fetches breath. Search his pockets.

He searcheth his pocket, and findeth certain papers.

What hast thou found?

Peto. Nothing but papers, my lord.

Prince. Let's see what they be. Read them.

Peto.

Item, a capon	2s. 2d.
Item, sauce	4d.
Item, sack, two gallons	5s. 8d.
Item, anchovies and sack after supper	2s. 6d.
Item, bread	ob.

Prince. O monstrous! but one halfpenny-worth of bread to this intolerable deal of sack? What there is else, keep close. We'll read it at more advantage. There let him sleep till day. I'll to the court in the morning. We must all to the wars, and thy place shall be honorable. I'll procure this fat rogue a charge

---

533 Paul's: *St. Paul's Cathedral*
546 ob.: *obolus = half-penny*
552 charge of foot: *command of infantry*

of foot, and I know his death will be a march of
twelve score. The money shall be paid back again
with advantage. Be with me betimes in the morning.
And so good morrow, Peto. 556
  Peto. Good morrow, good my lord. *Exeunt.*

ACT THIRD

SCENE FIRST

[Glendower's Castle in North Wales]

*Enter Hotspur, Worcester, Lord Mortimer,
Owen Glendower.*

  Mort. These promises are fair, the parties sure,
And our induction full of prosperous hope.
  Hot. Lord Mortimer, and Cousin Glendower,
Will you sit down? 4
And Uncle Worcester? A plague upon it,
I have forgot the map.
  Glend.   No, here it is.
Sit, Cousin Percy, sit, good Cousin Hotspur,
For by that name as oft as Lancaster 8
Doth speak of you, his cheek looks pale, and with
A rising sigh he wisheth you in heaven.
  Hot. And you in hell, as often as he hears
Owen Glendower spoke of. 12

554 twelve score: *240 yards of common archery range (cf. 2
    Henry IV, III. ii. 52)*
555 advantage: *interest*
2 induction: *beginning*   8 Lancaster: *the king*

Act III, Scene 1

Glend. I cannot blame him; at my nativity
The front of heaven was full of fiery shapes,
Of burning cressets, and at my birth
The frame and huge foundation of the earth   16
Shak'd like a coward.

    Hot. Why so it would have done at the same sea-
son if your mother's cat had but kittened, though
yourself had never been born.   20

    Glend. I say the earth did shake when I was born.

    Hot. And I say the earth was not of my mind,
If you suppose as fearing you it shook.

    Glend. The heavens were all on fire, the earth did
    tremble.   24

    Hot. O then th' earth shook to see the heavens on fire,
And not in fear of your nativity.
Diseased nature oftentimes breaks forth
In strange eruptions. Oft the teeming earth   28
Is with a kind of colic pinch'd and vex'd,
By the imprisoning of unruly wind
Within her womb, which for enlargement striving
Shakes the old beldam earth, and topples down   32
Steeples and mossgrown towers. At your birth
Our grandam earth, having this distemperature,
In passion shook.

    Glend.   Cousin, of many men
I do not bear these crossings. Give me leave   36
To tell you once again that at my birth
The front of heaven was full of fiery shapes,
The goats ran from the mountains, and the herds
Were strangely clamorous to the frighted fields.   40

---

15 cressets: *beacon lights*   31 enlargement: *release*
32 beldam: *grandmother*   35 passion: *pain*

These signs have mark'd me extraordinary,
And all the courses of my life do show
I am not in the roll of common men.
Where is he living, clipt in with the sea   44
That chides the banks of England, Scotland, Wales,
Which calls me pupil or hath read to me?
And bring him out that is but woman's son
Can trace me in the tedious ways of art,   48
And hold me pace in deep experiments.

  Hot. I think there's no man speaks better Welsh.
I'll to dinner.

  Mort. Peace, Cousin Percy, you will make him mad.

  Glend. I can call spirits from the vasty deep.   53

  Hot. Why so can I, or so can any man,
But will they come when you do call for them?

  Glend. Why I can teach you, cousin, to command   56
The devil.

  Hot. And I can teach thee, coz, to shame the devil,
By telling truth. Tell truth and shame the devil.
If thou have power to raise him bring him hither,   60
And I'll be sworn I have power to shame him hence.
O while you live tell truth and shame the devil!

  Mort. Come, come,
No more of this unprofitable chat.   64

  Glend. Three times hath Henry Bolingbroke made head
Against my power. Thrice from the banks of Wye
And sandy-bottom'd Severn have I sent him
Bootless home, and weather-beaten back.   68

---

44 clipt in with: *surrounded by*   45 chides: *lashes*
46 read to: *instructed*   48 trace: *follow*   art: *magic*
68 bootless: *without advantage; cf. I. i. 29*

Act III, Scene 1

Hot. Home without boots, and in foul weather too,
How 'scapes he agues, in the devil's name?
Glend. Come, here's the map. Shall we divide our right,
According to our threefold order ta'en? 72
Mort. The archdeacon hath divided it
Into three limits very equally.
England, from Trent and Severn hitherto,
By south and east, is to my part assign'd; 76
All westward, Wales beyond the Severn shore,
And all the fertile land within that bound
To Owen Glendower; and, dear coz, to you
The remnant northward, lying off from Trent. 80
And our indentures tripartite are drawn,
Which being sealed interchangeably,
A business that this night may execute,
To-morrow, Cousin Percy, you and I 84
And my good Lord of Worcester will set forth
To meet your father and the Scottish power,
As is appointed us, at Shrewsbury.
My father Glendower is not ready yet, 88
Nor shall we need his help these fourteen days.
[*To Glendower.*]
Within that space you may have drawn together
Your tenants, friends, and neighboring gentlemen.
Glend. A shorter time shall send me to you, lords, 92
And in my conduct shall your ladies come,
From whom you now must steal and take no leave,
For there will be a world of water shed,

73 The archdeacon; *cf. n.*
75 hitherto: *in this direction (i.e., south and east)*
81 indentures tripartite: *agreements between three parties*
82 interchangeably: *each party signing each copy*
93 conduct: *escort*

76   The First Part of Henry the Fourth

Upon the parting of your wives and you.   96
  Hot. Methinks my moiety, north from Burton here,
In quantity equals not one of yours.
See how this river comes me cranking in,
And cuts me from the best of all my land,   100
A huge half-moon, a monstrous cantle out.
I'll have the current in this place damm'd up,
And here the smug and silver Trent shall run
In a new channel, fair and evenly.   104
It shall not wind with such a deep indent,
To rob me of so rich a bottom here.
  Glend. Not wind? it shall! it must! You see it doth.
  Mort. Yea, but   108
Mark how he bears his course, and runs me up
With like advantage on the other side,
Gelding the opposed continent as much
As on the other side it takes from you.   112
  Wor. Yea, but a little charge will trench him here,
And on this north side win this cape of land,
And then he runs straight and even.
  Hot. I'll have it so. A little charge will do it.   116
  Glend. I'll not have it alter'd.
  Hot.   Will not you?
  Glend. No, nor you shall not.
  Hot.   Who shall say me nay?
  Glend. Why that will I.
  Hot.   Let me not understand you then.
Speak it in Welsh.   120

---

97 moiety: *portion*   99 cranking: *winding*
100 the best of all my land; *cf. n.*   101 cantle: *piece*
103 smug: *neat, trim*   106 bottom: *low, rich land*
111 Gelding: *cutting*   opposed continent: *country opposite*
113 charge: *expense*

Act III, Scene 1

Glend. I can speak English, lord, as well as you,
For I was train'd up in the English court,
Where, being but young, I framed to the harp
Many an English ditty lovely well,   124
And gave the tongue a helpful ornament,
A virtue that was never seen in you.

Hot. Marry,
And I am glad of it with all my heart.   128
I had rather be a kitten and cry mew,
Than one of these same meter ballet-mongers.
I had rather hear a brazen canstick turn'd,
Or a dry wheel grate on the axletree,   132
And that would set my teeth nothing on edge,
Nothing so much as mincing poetry;
'Tis like the forc'd gait of a shuffling nag.

Glend. Come, you shall have Trent turn'd.   136

Hot. I do not care. I'll give thrice so much land
To any well-deserving friend.
But in the way of bargain, mark ye me,
I'll cavil on the ninth part of a hair.   140
Are the indentures drawn? Shall we be gone?

Glend. The moon shines fair. You may away by night.
I'll haste the writer, and withal
Break with your wives of your departure hence.   144
I am afraid my daughter will run mad,
So much she doteth on her Mortimer.   *Exit.*

Mort. Fie, Cousin Percy, how you cross my father!

Hot. I cannot choose. Sometime he angers me   148
With telling me of the moldwarp and the ant,

---

125 Cf. *n.*   131 canstick: candlestick
134 mincing: *affected*   144 Break with: *inform*
148 cannot choose: *have no choice*   149–153 Cf. *n.*

78 The First Part of Henry the Fourth

Of the dreamer Merlin and his prophecies,
And of a dragon and a finless fish,
A clip-wing'd griffin and a moulten raven, 152
A couching lion and a ramping cat,
And such a deal of skimble-skamble stuff,
As puts me from my faith. I tell you what;
He held me last night at least nine hours 156
In reckoning up the several devils' names
That were his lackeys. I cried 'hum!' and 'Well, go to,'
But mark'd him not a word. O he is as tedious
As a tired horse, a railing wife, 160
Worse than a smoky house. I had rather live
With cheese and garlic in a windmill, far,
Than feed on cates and have him talk to me,
In any summer-house in Christendom. 164
  Mort. In faith he is a worthy gentleman,
Exceedingly well read and profited
In strange concealments, valiant as a lion,
And wondrous affable; and as bountiful 168
As mines of India. Shall I tell you, cousin,
He holds your temper in a high respect,
And curbs himself even of his natural scope
When you come cross his humor; faith he does. 172
I warrant you that man is not alive
Might so have tempted him as you have done
Without the taste of danger and reproof.
But do not use it oft, let me entreat you. 176
  Wor. In faith, my lord, you are too wilful-blame,

154 skimble-skamble: *nonsensical*   163 cates: *dainties*
164 summer-house: *country pleasure-house*
166 profited: *proficient*
167 concealments: *mysteries*   171 scope: *tendencies*
177 too wilful-blame: *to be blamed for too great wilfulness*

Act III, Scene 1

And since your coming hither have done enough
To put him quite besides his patience.
You must needs learn, lord, to amend this fault. 180
Though sometimes it show greatness, courage, blood,
And that's the dearest grace it renders you,
Yet often times it doth present harsh rage,
Defect of manners, want of government, 184
Pride, haughtiness, opinion, and disdain—
The least of which haunting a nobleman
Loseth men's hearts and leaves behind a stain
Upon the beauty of all parts besides, 188
Beguiling them of commendation.

Hot. Well, I am school'd. Good manners be your speed!
Here come our wives, and let us take our leave.

Enter Glendower with the Ladies.

Mort. This is the deadly spite that angers me, 192
My wife can speak no English, I no Welsh.

Glend. My daughter weeps. She'll not part with you.
She'll be a soldier too, she'll to the wars.

Mort. Good father, tell her that she and my Aunt Percy
Shall follow in your conduct speedily. 197

*Glendower speaks to her in Welsh, and she
answers him in the same.*

Glend. She is desperate here, a peevish self-will'd
harlotry, one that no persuasion can do good upon.

---

179 quite besides: *completely out of*
181 blood: *spirit*   182 dearest: *most valuable*
183 present: *indicate*   184 government: *self-control*
185 opinion: *arrogance*   189 Beguiling: *cheating*
190 be your speed: *bring you good fortune*
196 Aunt; *cf. n. on* I. iii. 145, 146
199 harlotry: *silly girl*

80 The First Part of Henry the Fourth

The lady speaks in Welsh.

Mort. I understand thy looks. That pretty Welsh 200
Which thou pour'st down from these swelling heavens
I am too perfect in, and but for shame,
In such a parley should I answer thee.

The lady again in Welsh.

I understand thy kisses, and thou mine, 204
And that's a feeling disputation.
But I will never be a truant, love,
Till I have learnt thy language, for thy tongue
Makes Welsh as sweet as ditties highly penn'd, 208
Sung by a fair queen in a summer's bower,
With ravishing division, to her lute.

Glend. Nay, if you melt, then will she run mad.

The lady speaks again in Welsh.

Mort. O I am ignorance itself in this. 212
Glend. She bids you
On the wanton rushes lay you down,
And rest your gentle head upon her lap,
And she will sing the song that pleaseth you, 216
And on your eyelids crown the god of sleep,
Charming your blood with pleasing heaviness,
Making such difference 'twixt wake and sleep,
As is the difference betwixt day and night, 220
The hour before the heavenly-harness'd team
Begins his golden progress in the east.

Mort. With all my heart I'll sit and hear her sing.
By that time will our book, I think, be drawn. 224

200–203 *Cf. n.*   205 disputation: *conversation*
208 highly penn'd: *written in high style*
210 division: *modulation*   214 wanton: *soft, luxurious*
224 book: *document, indentures*

Act III, Scene 1

Glend. Do so,
And those musicians that shall play to you
Hang in the air a thousand leagues from hence,
And straight they shall be here. Sit, and attend. 228

Hot. Come, Kate, thou art perfect in lying down.
Come, quick, quick, that I may lay my head in thy lap.

Lady P. Go, ye giddy goose. 232
The music plays.

Hot. Now I perceive the devil understands Welsh,
And 'tis no marvel he is so humorous.
By'r lady, he's a good musician. 235

Lady P. Then should you be nothing but musical, for you are altogether governed by humors. Lie still, ye thief, and hear the lady sing in Welsh.

Hot. I had rather hear Lady my brach howl in Irish. 240

Lady P. Wouldst thou have thy head broken?
Hot. No.
Lady P. Then be still.
Hot. Neither; 'tis a woman's fault. 244
Lady P. Now God help thee!
Hot. To the Welsh lady's bed.
Lady P. What's that?
Hot. Peace, she sings. 248
Here the lady sings a Welsh song.

Hot. Come, Kate, I'll have your song too.
Lady P. Not mine, in good sooth.
Hot. Not yours, 'in good sooth!' Heart, you swear

230, 231 head . . . lap; *cf. Hamlet III. ii. 112–114*
234 he: *because he*   humorous: *capricious, queer*
239 brach: *a bitch-hound*

like a comfit-maker's wife. 'Not you in good sooth,'
and 'as true as I live,' and 'as God shall mend me,'
and 'as sure as day': and giv'st such sarcenet surety
for thy oaths, as if thou never walk'st further than
Finsbury. Swear me, Kate, like a lady as thou art,
a good mouth-filling oath, and leave 'in sooth,' and
such protest of pepper-gingerbread, to velvet-guards
and Sunday-citizens. Come, sing.

Lady P. I will not sing.   260

Hot. 'Tis the next way to turn tailor, or be redbreast-teacher. An the indentures be drawn, I'll away
within these two hours, and so, come in when ye
will.
                                                    Exit.

Glend. Come, come, Lord Mortimer. You are as slow
As hot Lord Percy is on fire to go.
By this our book is drawn. We'll but seal, and then
to horse immediately.   268

Mort. With all my heart.   *Exeunt.*

SCENE SECOND

[*Westminster. The Palace*]

Enter the King, Prince of Wales, and others.

King. Lords, give us leave. The Prince of Wales and I
Must have some private conference. But be near at hand,
For we shall presently have need of you.

                                            Exeunt Lords.

252 comfit-maker: *confectioner*　　　254 sarcenet: *flimsy*
256 Finsbury; *cf. n.*　　　258 velvet-guards; *cf. n.*
261 tailor; *cf. n.*　　redbreast-teacher: *trainer of singing-birds*
1 give us leave: *leave us*　　　3 presently: *immediately*

Act III, Scene 2   83

I know not whether God will have it so,   4
For some displeasing service I have done,
That in his secret doom out of my blood
He'll breed revengement and a scourge for me.
But thou dost in thy passages of life,   8
Make me believe that thou art only mark'd
For the hot vengeance, and the rod of heaven,
To punish my mistreadings. Tell me else,
Could such inordinate and low desires,   12
Such poor, such bare, such lewd, such mean attempts,
Such barren pleasures, rude society,
As thou art match'd withal, and grafted to,
Accompany the greatness of thy blood,   16
And hold their level with thy princely heart?
  Prince. So please your majesty, I would I could
Quit all offences with as clear excuse,
As well, as I am doubtless I can purge   20
Myself of many I am charg'd withal.
Yet such extenuation let me beg,
As in reproof of many tales devis'd,
Which oft the ear of greatness needs must hear   24
By smiling pickthanks and base newsmongers,
I may, for some things true, wherein my youth
Hath faulty wander'd, and irregular,
Find pardon on my true submission.   28
  King. God pardon thee! yet let me wonder, Harry,

---

6 doom: *judgment*
8 thy passages of life: *the actions of thy life*
19 Quit: *clear myself of*
20 As well: *and as well*   doubtless: *positive, without doubt*
22 extenuation: *mitigation of censure*
23–28 Cf. *n.*

84   The First Part of Henry the Fourth

At thy affections, which do hold a wing
Quite from the flight of all thy ancestors.
Thy place in council thou hast rudely lost,   32
Which by thy younger brother is supplied,
And art almost an alien to the hearts
Of all the court and princes of my blood.
The hope and expectation of thy time   36
Is ruin'd, and the soul of every man
Prophetically do forethink thy fall.
Had I so lavish of my presence been,
So common-hackney'd in the eyes of men,   40
So stale and cheap to vulgar company,
Opinion, that did help me to the crown,
Had still kept loyal to possession,
And left me in reputeless banishment,   44
A fellow of no mark nor likelihood.
By being seldom seen, I could not stir
But like a comet I was wonder'd at;
That men would tell their children 'This is he.'   48
Others would say, 'Where? which is Bolingbroke?'
And then I stole all courtesy from heaven,
And dress'd myself in such humility
That I did pluck allegiance from men's hearts,   52
Loud shouts, and salutations from their mouths,
Even in the presence of the crowned king.
Thus did I keep my person fresh and new,
My presence like a robe pontifical,   56
Ne'er seen but wonder'd at; and so my state,

30 affections: *tastes*   hold a wing: *take a course*
31 from the flight: *unlike the direction*
36 time: *age, reign*   42 Opinion: *public opinion*
43 to possession: *to the possessor, i.e., King Richard*
48, 70 That: *so that*   50 stole, etc.; *cf. n.*

Act III, Scene 2

Seldom, but sumptuous, showed like a feast,
And wan by rareness such solemnity.
The skipping king, he ambled up and down, 60
With shallow jesters, and rash bavin wits,
Soon kindled, and soon burnt, carded his state,
Mingled his royalty with cap'ring fools,
Had his great name profaned with their scorns, 64
And gave his countenance, against his name,
To laugh at gibing boys, and stand the push
Of every beardless vain comparative,
Grew a companion to the common streets, 68
Enfeoff'd himself to popularity,
That being daily swallow'd by men's eyes,
They surfeited with honey, and began
To loathe the taste of sweetness, whereof a little 72
More than a little is by much too much.
So when he had occasion to be seen,
He was but as the cuckoo is in June,
Heard, not regarded; seen, but with such eyes 76
As, sick and blunted with community,
Afford no extraordinary gaze,
Such as is bent on sun-like majesty,
When it shines seldom in admiring eyes, 80
But rather drows'd, and hung their eyelids down,
Slept in his face, and render'd such aspéct

---

59 wan: *won*
61 bavin: *brushwood, which soon burns out*
62 carded; *cf. n.*   65 against his name: *contrary to his dignity*
66 stand the push: *face the competition*
67 comparative: *one who affects wit; cf. I. ii. 83*
69 Enfeoff'd himself: *gave himself up entirely*   popularity: *low company*
77 community: *commonness*

86 The First Part of Henry the Fourth

As cloudy men use to their adversaries,
Being with his presence glutted, gorg'd, and full. 84
And in that very line, Harry, standest thou,
For thou hast lost thy princely privilege
With vile participation. Not an eye
But is aweary of thy common sight, 88
Save mine, which hath desir'd to see thee more—
Which now doth that I would not have it do,
Make blind itself with foolish tenderness.

Prince. I shall hereafter, my thrice gracious lord, 92
Be more myself.

King.   For all the world,
As thou art to this hour was Richard then,
When I from France set foot at Ravenspurgh,
And even as I was then, is Percy now. 96
Now, by my scepter, and my soul to boot,
He hath more worthy interest to the state
Than thou the shadow of succession.
For of no right, nor color like to right, 100
He doth fill fields with harness in the realm,
Turns head against the lion's armed jaws,
And, being no more in debt to years than thou,
Leads ancient lords and reverend bishops on 104
To bloody battles, and to bruising arms.
What never-dying honor hath he got
Against renowned Douglas! whose high deeds,
Whose hot incursions, and great name in arms, 108
Holds from all soldiers chief majority

---

83 cloudy: *sullen*
87 vile participation: *base companionship*
98 interest: *claim*
99 shadow of succession; *cf. n.*
100 color: *pretext*
101 harness: *armed men*
103 *Cf. n.*
109 majority: *pre-eminence*

Act III, Scene 2

And military title capital
Through all the kingdoms that acknowledge Christ.
Thrice hath this Hotspur, Mars in swathling clothes, 112
This infant warrior, in his enterprises
Discomfited great Douglas, ta'en him once,
Enlarged him, and made a friend of him,
To fill the mouth of deep defiance up, 116
And shake the peace and safety of our throne.
And what say you to this? Percy, Northumberland,
The Archbishop's Grace of York, Douglas, Mortimer,
Capitulate against us, and are up. 120
But wherefore do I tell these news to thee?
Why, Harry, do I tell thee of my foes,
Which art my near'st and dearest enemy?
Thou that art like enough through vassal fear, 124
Base inclination, and the start of spleen,
To fight against me under Percy's pay,
To dog his heels, and curtsy at his frowns,
To show how much thou art degenerate. 128
  Prince. Do not think so. You shall not find it so.
And God forgive them that so much have sway'd
Your majesty's good thoughts away from me.
I will redeem all this on Percy's head, 132
And in the closing of some glorious day
Be bold to tell you that I am your son,
When I will wear a garment all of blood,
And stain my favors in a bloody mask, 136
Which, wash'd away, shall scour my shame with it.

---

110 capital: *chief*
115 Enlarged: *released*
120 Capitulate: *form a league*
124 vassal: *slavish*
125 start of spleen: *impulse of ill temper*
136 favors: *features*

88 The First Part of Henry the Fourth

And that shall be the day, whene'er it lights,
That this same child of honor and renown,
This gallant Hotspur, this all-praised knight, 140
And your unthought-of Harry chance to meet.
For every honor sitting on his helm,
Would they were multitudes, and on my head
My shames redoubled. For the time will come 144
That I shall make this Northern youth exchange
His glorious deeds for my indignities.
Percy is but my factor, good my lord,
To engross up glorious deeds on my behalf. 148
And I will call him to so strict account,
That he shall render every glory up,
Yea, even the slightest worship of his time,
Or I will tear the reckoning from his heart. 152
This in the name of God I promise here,
The which if he be pleas'd I shall perform,
I do beseech your majesty may salve
The long-grown wounds of my intemperance. 156
If not, the end of life cancels all bands,
And I will die a hundred thousand deaths
Ere break the smallest parcel of this vow.
    King. A hundred thousand rebels die in this. 160
Thou shalt have charge and sovereign trust herein.

Enter Blunt.

How now, good Blunt! Thy looks are full of speed.
    Blunt. So hath the business that I come to speak of.
Lord Mortimer of Scotland hath sent word, 164

147 factor: *agent*   148 engross up: *buy up*
151 worship: *distinction*   157 bands: *bonds*
164 Lord Mortimer of Scotland; *cf. n.*

Act III, Scene 2

That Douglas and the English rebels met
The eleventh of this month at Shrewsbury.
A mighty and a fearful head they are,
If promises be kept on every hand, 168
As ever offer'd foul play in a state.

King. The Earl of Westmorland set forth to-day,
With him my son, Lord John of Lancaster,
For this advertisement is five days old. 172
On Wednesday next, Harry, you shall set forward.
On Thursday we ourselves will march. Our meeting
Is Bridgenorth, and Harry, you shall march
Through Gloucestershire, by which account, 176
Our business valued, some twelve days hence
Our general forces at Bridgenorth shall meet.
Our hands are full of business, let's away.
Advantage feeds him fat while men delay. 180

Exeunt.

SCENE THIRD

[*Eastcheap. The Boar's Head Tavern*]

Enter Falstaff and Bardolph.

Fal. Bardolph, am I not fallen away vilely since this last action? Do I not bate? Do I not dwindle? Why, my skin hangs about me like an old lady's loose gown. I am withered like an old apple-john.

---

172 advertisement: *information*   174 meeting: *rendezvous*
177 valued: *taken into consideration*
2 bate: *fall off, grow thin*
4 apple-john: *an apple that keeps well but becomes very shrivelled*

Well, I'll repent, and that suddenly, while I am in some liking. I shall be out of heart shortly, and then I shall have no strength to repent. An I have not forgotten what the inside of a church is made of, I am a peppercorn, a brewer's horse. The inside of a church? Company, villainous company, hath been the spoil of me.

Bard. Sir John, you are so fretful you cannot live long. 13

Fal. Why, there is it! Come sing me a bawdy song, make me merry. I was as virtuously given as a gentleman need to be; virtuous enough, swore little, diced not above seven times a week, went to a bawdy-house not above once in a quarter—of an hour, paid money that I borrowed—three or four times, lived well, and in good compass. And now I live out of all order, out of all compass. 21

Bard. Why, you are so fat, Sir John, that you must needs be out of all compass; out of all reasonable compass, Sir John. 24

Fal. Do thou amend thy face, and I'll amend my life. Thou art our admiral, thou bearest the lantern in the poop, but 'tis in the nose of thee. Thou art the Knight of the Burning Lamp. 28

Bard. Why, Sir John, my face does you no harm.

Fal. No, I'll be sworn. I make as good use of it as many a man doth of a death's head, or a *memento mori*. I never see thy face, but I think upon hell-fire,

---

6 liking: (good) *bodily condition*
9 peppercorn: *the dried berry from which pepper is ground*
brewer's horse; *cf. n.*
26 admiral: *flagship*   31 *memento mori; cf. n.*

Act III, Scene 3

and Dives that lived in purple: for there he is in his
robes, burning, burning. If thou wert any way given
to virtue, I would swear by thy face: my oath should
be, 'By this fire that's God's angel.' But thou art
altogether given over: and wert indeed, but for the
light in thy face, the son of utter darkness. When
thou ran'st up Gadshill in the night to catch my
horse, if I did not think thou hadst been an *ignis
fatuus*, or a ball of wildfire, there's no purchase in
money. O thou art a perpetual triumph, an ever-
lasting bonfire-light! Thou hast saved me a thousand
marks in links and torches, walking with thee in the
night betwixt tavern and tavern; but the sack that
thou hast drunk me would have bought me lights as
good cheap at the dearest chandler's in Europe. I
have maintained that salamander of yours with fire
any time this two and thirty years, God reward me
for it! 50

Bard. 'Sblood, I would my face were in your belly.

Fal. God-a-mercy! so should I be sure to be heart-
burned.

Enter Hostess.

How now, Dame Partlet the hen! Have you inquired
yet who picked my pocket? 55

Host. Why Sir John, what do you think, Sir
John? Do you think I keep thieves in my house? I

---

33 Dives; *cf. n.*   36 God's angel; *cf. n.*
40 *ignis fatuus*: will o' the wisp
42 triumph: *festive celebration*   44 links: *street lights*
46 as good cheap: *at as good a bargain*
48 salamander: *mythical animal supposed to live in fire*
54 Partlet; *cf. n.*

92   The First Part of Henry the Fourth

have searched, I have inquired, so has my husband, man by man, boy by boy, servant by servant. The tithe of a hair was never lost in my house before.   60

Fal. Ye lie, hostess. Bardolph was shaved, and lost many a hair, and I'll be sworn my pocket was picked. Go to, you are a woman! Go.

Host. Who, I? No. I defy thee. God's light! I was never called so in mine own house before.   65

Fal. Go to! I know you well enough.

Host. No, Sir John, you do not know me, Sir John. I know you, Sir John. You owe me money, Sir John, and now you pick a quarrel to beguile me of it. I bought you a dozen of shirts to your back.   70

Fal. Dowlas, filthy dowlas. I have given them away to bakers' wives, and they have made bolters of them.

Host. Now as I am a true woman, holland of eight shillings an ell! You owe money here besides, Sir John, for your diet, and by-drinkings, and money lent you, four and twenty pound.   76

Fal. He had his part of it. Let him pay.

Host. He? alas! he is poor. He hath nothing.

Fal. How? poor? Look upon his face. What call you rich? Let them coin his nose, let them coin his cheeks. I'll not pay a denier. What? will you make a younker of me? Shall I not take mine ease in mine inn, but I shall have my pocket picked? I have lost a seal-ring of my grandfather's worth forty mark.   84

---

60 tithe: *tenth part; cf. n.*   71 dowlas: *coarse linen*
72 bolters: *sieves*   73 holland: *fine linen*
74 ell: *yard and a quarter*
81 denier: *the tenth part of a penny*
82 younker: *young greenhorn*

Act III, Scene 3

Host. O Jesu, I have heard the prince tell him, I know not how oft, that that ring was copper.

Fal. How? the prince is a Jack, a sneak-up, 'Sblood! an he were here, I would cudgel him like a dog if he would say so. 89

Enter the Prince marching [with Peto], and Falstaff meets him, playing upon his truncheon like a fife.

Fal. How now, lad? is the wind in that door, i' faith? Must we all march?

Bard. Yea, two and two, Newgate fashion. 92

Host. My lord, I pray you hear me.

Prince. What sayest thou, Mistress Quickly? How doth thy husband? I love him well. He is an honest man. 96

Host. Good my lord, hear me.

Fal. Prithee let her alone, and list to me.

Prince. What say'st thou, Jack?

Fal. The other night I fell asleep here, behind the arras, and had my pocket picked. This house is turned bawdy-house, they pick pockets. 102

Prince. What didst thou lose, Jack?

Fal. Wilt thou believe me, Hal? Three or four bonds of forty pound apiece, and a seal-ring of my grandfather's. 106

Prince. A trifle. Some eightpenny matter.

Host. So I told him, my lord, and I said I heard your Grace say so. And, my lord, he speaks most vilely of you, like a foul-mouthed man as he is, and said he would cudgel you.

---

87 sneak-up: *shirker*   89 S. d. truncheon: *officer's baton*
92 Newgate: *a prison*

Prince. What? he did not!

Host. There's neither faith, truth, nor womanhood in me else.

Fal. There's no more faith in thee than in a stewed prune, nor no more truth in thee than in a drawn fox, and for womanhood, Maid Marian may be the deputy's wife of the ward to thee. Go, you thing, go!

Host. Say, what thing? what thing?

Fal. What thing? Why, a thing to thank God on.

Host. I am no thing to thank God on, I would thou shouldst know it! I am an honest man's wife, and setting thy knighthood aside, thou art a knave to call me so.

Fal. Setting thy womanhood aside, thou art a beast to say otherwise.

Host. Say, what beast, thou knave thou?

Fal. What beast? Why, an otter.

Prince. An otter, Sir John? why an otter?

Fal. Why? She's neither fish nor flesh; a man knows not where to have her.

Host. Thou art an unjust man in saying so. Thou or any man knows where to have me, thou knave thou!

Prince. Thou say'st true, hostess, and he slanders thee most grossly.

Host. So he doth you, my lord, and said this other day you ought him a thousand pound.

Prince. Sirrah, do I owe you a thousand pound?

---

116 drawn fox: *a fox driven from cover and tricky in his attempts to get back*
117 Cf. *n.*   139 ought: *owed*

Act III, Scene 3

Fal. A thousand pound, Hal? a million. Thy love is worth a million. Thou owest me thy love.

Host. Nay my lord, he called you Jack, and said he would cudgel you. 144

Fal. Did I, Bardolph?

Bard. Indeed, Sir John, you said so.

Fal. Yea, if he said my ring was copper.

Prince. I say 'tis copper. Darest thou be as good as thy word now? 149

Fal. Why, Hal, thou knowest, as thou art but man, I dare. But as thou art prince, I fear thee as I fear the roaring of the lion's whelp. 152

Prince. And why not as the lion?

Fal. The king himself is to be feared as the lion. Dost thou think I'll fear thee as I fear thy father? Nay an I do, I pray God my girdle break. 156

Prince. O, if it should, how would thy guts fall about thy knees! But sirrah, there's no room for faith, truth, nor honesty, in this bosom of thine. It is all filled up with guts and midriff. Charge an honest woman with picking thy pocket! Why, thou whoreson, impudent, embossed rascal, if there were anything in thy pocket but tavern reckonings, memorandums of bawdy-houses, and one poor pennyworth of sugar-candy to make thee long-winded—if thy pocket were enriched with any other injuries but these, I am a villain. And yet you will stand to it, you will not pocket up wrong. Art thou not ashamed? 168

Fal. Dost thou hear, Hal? Thou knowest in the state of innocency Adam fell, and what should poor Jack Falstaff do in the days of villainy? Thou seest

162 embossed: *swollen*   166 injuries; *cf. n.*

I have more flesh than another man, and therefore more frailty. You confess then you picked my pocket?

Prince. It appears so by the story.

Fal. Hostess, I forgive thee. Go make ready breakfast, love thy husband, look to thy servants, cherish thy guests. Thou shalt find me tractable to any honest reason. Thou seest I am pacified still. Nay, prithee be gone.

Exit Hostess.

Now Hal, to the news at court. For the robbery, lad? How is that answered?

Prince. O my sweet beef, I must still be good angel to thee. The money is paid back again.

Fal. O I do not like that paying back. 'Tis a double labor.

Prince. I am good friends with my father and may do anything.

Fal. Rob me the exchequer the first thing thou dost, and do it with unwashed hands too.

Bard. Do, my lord!

Prince. I have procured thee, Jack, a charge of foot.

Fal. I would it had been of horse. Where shall I find one that can steal well? O for a fine thief of the age of two and twenty or thereabouts! I am heinously unprovided. Well, God be thanked for these rebels. They offend none but the virtuous. I laud them, I praise them.

Prince. Bardolph!

Bard. My lord?

190 unwashed hands; *cf. n.*

Prince. Go bear this letter to Lord John of Lancaster, to my brother John; this to my Lord of Westmorland. Go, Peto, to horse, to horse! for thou and I have thirty miles to ride yet ere dinner-time. Jack, meet me to-morrow in the Temple-hall at two o'clock in the afternoon. There shalt thou know thy charge, and there receive money and order for their furniture. 209
The land is burning, Percy stands on high,
And either we or they must lower lie.
Fal. Rare words! brave world! Hostess, my breakfast; come!
O, I could wish this tavern were my drum. 213
Exeunt omnes.

ACT FOURTH

SCENE FIRST

[*The Rebel Camp near Shrewsbury*]

Enter Harry Hotspur, Worcester, and Douglas.

Hot. Well said, my noble Scot! If speaking truth
In this fine age were not thought flattery,
Such attribution should the Douglas have
As not a soldier of this season's stamp 4

---

208 furniture: *equipment*
213 drum; *cf. n.*
3 attribution: *credit*

2 fine: *sophisticated*
4, 5 Cf. *n.*

98 The First Part of Henry the Fourth

Should go so general current through the world.
By God, I cannot flatter. I do defy
The tongues of soothers. But a braver place
In my heart's love hath no man than yourself. 8
Nay, task me to my word. Approve me, lord.

  Doug. Thou art the king of honor.
No man so potent breathes upon the ground
But I will beard him.

  Hot.   Do so, and 'tis well— 12

Enter one with letters.

What letters hast thou there?—[*To Doug.*] I can but thank you.

  Messenger. These letters come from your father.

  Hot. Letters from him? Why comes he not himself?

  Mess. He cannot come, my lord. He is grievous sick.

  Hot. 'Zounds! how has he the leisure to be sick 17
In such a justling time? Who leads his power?
Under whose government come they along?

  Mess. His letters bears his mind, not I, my lord. 20

  Wor. I prithee tell me, doth he keep his bed?

  Mess. He did, my lord, four days ere I set forth,
And at the time of my departure thence
He was much fear'd by his physicians. 24

  Wor. I would the state of time had first been whole
Ere he by sickness had been visited.
His health was never better worth than now.

  Hot. Sick now? droop now? This sickness doth infect

6 defy: *despise*   7 soothers: *flatterers*
9 task me to my word: *challenge me to make good my word*
  Approve: *test*
18 justling: *busy*

Act IV, Scene 1

The very life-blood of our enterprise.   29
'Tis catching hither, even to our camp.
He writes me here that inward sickness—
And that his friends by deputation could not   32
So soon be drawn, nor did he think it meet
To lay so dangerous and dear a trust
On any soul remov'd but on his own—
Yet doth he give us bold advertisement,   36
That with our small conjunction we should on,
To see how fortune is dispos'd to us;
For, as he writes, there is no quailing now,
Because the king is certainly possess'd   40
Of all our purposes. What say you to it?
  Wor. Your father's sickness is a maim to us.
  Hot. A perilous gash, a very limb lopp'd off.
And yet, in faith, it is not. His present want   44
Seems more than we shall find it. Were it good
To set the éxact wealth of all our states
All at one cast? to set so rich a main
On the nice hazard of one doubtful hour?   48
It were not good, for therein should we read
The very bottom and the soul of hope,
The very list, the very utmost bound
Of all our fortunes.   52
  Doug. Faith, and so we should, where now remains
A sweet reversion. We may boldly spend
Upon the hope of what is to come in.
A comfort of retirement lives in this.   56

---

36 advertisement: *advice* 37 conjunction: *united forces*
40 possess'd: *informed*   44 His present want: *his absence now*
47 main: *stake*   48 nice: *slender, precarious*
50 soul: *final essence*   51 list: *limit*
54 reversion: *right of future possession*   56 Cf. *n.*

Hot. A rendezvous, a home to fly unto,
If that the devil and mischance look big
Upon the maidenhead of our affairs.

Wor. But yet I would your father had been here. 60
The quality and hair of our attempt
Brooks no division. It will be thought
By some that know not why he is away,
That wisdom, loyalty, and mere dislike 64
Of our proceedings kept the earl from hence.
And think how such an apprehension
May turn the tide of fearful faction,
And breed a kind of question in our cause. 68
For well you know we of the offering side
Must keep aloof from strict arbitrement,
And stop all sight-holes, every loop from whence
The eye of reason may pry in upon us. 72
This absence of your father's draws a curtain,
That shows the ignorant a kind of fear
Before not dreamt of.

Hot. You strain too far.
I rather of his absence make this use: 76
It lends a lustre and more great opinion,
A larger dare to our great enterprise,
Than if the earl were here. For men must think,
If we without his help can make a head 80
To push against a kingdom, with his help
We shall o'erturn it topsy-turvy down.
Yet all goes well, yet all our joints are whole.

58 big: *threateningly* 61 hair: *nature*
67 fearful: *timid*   69 the offering side: *the offensive*
70 arbitrement: *judicial inquiry*   71 loop: *loophole*
73 draws: *draws aside*   77 opinion: *prestige*

Act IV, Scene 1

Doug. As heart can think! There is not such a word
Spoke of in Scotland as this term of fear. 85

Enter Sir Richard Vernon.

Hot. My cousin Vernon! Welcome, by my soul.
Ver. Pray God my news be worth a welcome, lord.
The Earl of Westmorland, seven thousand strong, 88
Is marching hitherwards, with him Prince John.
Hot. No harm. What more?
Ver. And further I have learn'd,
The king himself in person is set forth,
Or hitherwards intended speedily 92
With strong and mighty preparation.
Hot. He shall be welcome too. Where is his son,
The nimble-footed madcap Prince of Wales,
And his comrádes that daff'd the world aside 96
And bid it pass?
Ver. All furnish'd, all in arms,
All plum'd like estriges that woo the wind;
Bating like eagles having lately bath'd,
Glittering in golden coats like images, 100
As full of spirit as the month of May,
And gorgeous as the sun at midsummer:
Wanton as youthful goats, wild as young bulls.
I saw young Harry with his beaver on, 104
His cushes on his thighs, gallantly arm'd,
Rise from the ground like feather'd Mercury,
And vaulted with such ease into his seat,

---

96 daff'd: *thrust* 97 furnish'd: *equipped*
98 estriges: *ostriches; cf. n.*
99 Bating: *flapping their wings (falconry term); cf. n.*
100 *Cf. n.* 101 *Cf. n.*
104 beaver: *helmet* 105 cushes: *cuisses, thigh-armor*

102   The First Part of Henry the Fourth

As if an angel dropp'd down from the clouds, 108
To turn and wind a fiery Pegasus,
And witch the world with noble horsemanship.
   Hot. No more, no more. Worse than the sun in March
This praise doth nourish agues. Let them come! 112
They come like sacrifices in their trim,
And to the fire-ey'd maid of smoky war,
All hot and bleeding will we offer them.
The mailed Mars shall on his altar sit 116
Up to the ears in blood. I am on fire
To hear this rich reprisal is so nigh,
And yet not ours. Come let me taste my horse,
Who is to bear me like a thunderbolt 120
Against the bosom of the Prince of Wales.
Harry to Harry shall, hot horse to horse,
Meet and ne'er part till one drop down a corse.
O that Glendower were come!
   Ver.   There is more news. 124
I learn'd in Worcester as I rode along,
He cannot draw his power this fourteen days.
   Doug. That's the worst tidings that I hear of yet.
   Wor. Ay by my faith, that bears a frosty sound. 128
   Hot. What may the king's whole battle reach unto?
   Ver. To thirty thousand.
   Hot.   Forty let it be.
My father and Glendower being both away,
The powers of us may serve so great a day. 132
Come let us take a muster speedily.
Doomsday is near, die all, die merrily.

---

109 wind: *wheel round*
111, 112 Cf. *n.*   113 trim: *trappings*
114 fire-ey'd maid; *cf. n.*   118 reprisal: *prize*

Act IV, Scene 1

Doug. Talk not of dying. I am out of fear
Of death or death's hand for this one half-year.
Exeunt omnes.

SCENE SECOND

[*Warwickshire. A Road near Coventry*]

Enter Falstaff and Bardolph.

Fal. Bardolph, get thee before to Coventry. Fill me a bottle of sack. Our soldiers shall march through. We'll to Sutton Cophill to-night.

Bard. Will you give me money, captain?

Fal. Lay out, lay out.

Bard. This bottle makes an angel.

Fal. And if it do, take it for thy labor. And if it make twenty take them all; I'll answer the coinage. Bid my lieutenant Peto meet me at town's end.

Bard. I will, captain. Farewell. *Exit.*

Fal. If I be not ashamed of my soldiers, I am a soused gurnet. I have misused the king's press damnably. I have got, in exchange of a hundred and fifty soldiers, three hundred and odd pounds. I press me none but good householders, yeomen's sons; inquire me out contracted bachelors, such as had been asked twice on the banes—such a commodity of warm

3 Sutton Cophill; *cf. n.* 6 makes an angel; *cf. n.*
8 answer the coinage; *cf. n.*
12 soused gurnet: *pickled fish* king's press: *royal warrant for conscripting troops; cf. n.*
15 yeomen's: *small freeholders'*
17 banes: *marriage banns* warm: *luxury-loving*

104   The First Part of Henry the Fourth

slaves, as had as lief hear the devil as a drum, such as fear the report of a caliver worse than a struck fowl or a hurt wild duck. I pressed me none but such toasts-and-butter, with hearts in their bellies no bigger than pins' heads, and they have bought out their services, and now my whole charge consists of ancients, corporals, lieutenants, gentlemen of companies: slaves as ragged as Lazarus in the painted cloth, where the glutton's dogs licked his sores, and such as indeed were never soldiers, but discarded, unjust serving-men, younger sons to younger brothers, revolted tapsters and ostlers trade-fallen, the cankers of a calm world and a long peace, ten times more dishonorable ragged than an old faz'd ancient. And such have I to fill up the rooms of them as have bought out their services, that you would think that I had a hundred and fifty tottered prodigals, lately come from swine-keeping, from eating draff and husks. A mad fellow met me on the way, and told me I had unloaded all the gibbets, and pressed the dead bodies. No eye hath seen such scarecrows. I'll not march through Coventry with them, that's flat. Nay, and the villains march wide betwixt the legs, as if they had gyves on, for indeed I had the most of them out of prison. There's but a shirt and a half in all my company, and the half shirt is two napkins

---

19 caliver: *musket*   23 ancients: *ensigns*
25 Lazarus; *cf. III. iii. 33, n.*   painted cloth: *hanging decorated with figures*
30 cankers: *caterpillars*
31 faz'd: *feazed, unraveled*   ancient: *flag*   32 as: *who*
34 tottered: *tattered*   prodigals; *cf. n.*   35 draff: *pig-wash*
41 gyves: *fetters*
42 but; *cf. n.*

Act IV, Scene 2

tacked together, and thrown over the shoulders like a herald's coat without sleeves, and the shirt, to say the truth, stolen from my host at Saint Alban's, or the red-nose inn-keeper of Daventry. But that's all one, they'll find linen enough on every hedge. 48

Enter the Prince, and the Lord of Westmorland.

Prince. How now, blown Jack? how now, quilt?

Fal. What, Hal? How now, mad wag? What a devil dost thou in Warwickshire? My good Lord of Westmorland, I cry you mercy. I thought your honor had already been at Shrewsbury. 53

West. Faith, Sir John, 'tis more than time that I were there, and you too, but my powers are there already. The king, I can tell you, looks for us all. We must away all night. 57

Fal. Tut, never fear me. I am as vigilant as a cat to steal cream.

Prince. I think to steal cream indeed, for thy theft hath already made thee butter. But tell me, Jack, whose fellows are these that come after?

Fal. Mine, Hal, mine.

Prince. I did never see such pitiful rascals. 64

Fal. Tut, tut! Good enough to toss, food for powder, food for powder. They'll fill a pit as well as better; tush, man, mortal men, mortal men.

West. Ay, but Sir John, methinks they are exceeding poor and bare, too beggarly. 69

Fal. Faith, for their poverty I know not where they had that, and for their bareness I am sure they never learned that of me. 72

---

49 blown: *swollen*   65 to toss: *i.e., upon a pike*

Prince. No, I'll be sworn, unless you call three fingers in the ribs bare. But sirrah, make haste. Percy is already in the field.

Fal. What, is the king encamped? 76

West. He is, Sir John. I fear we shall stay too long.

Fal. Well, to the latter end of a fray, and the beginning of a feast, fits a dull fighter and a keen guest.

Exeunt.

SCENE THIRD

[*The Rebel Camp near Shrewsbury*]

Enter Hotspur, Worcester, Douglas, and Vernon.

Hot. We'll fight with him to-night.
Wor. It may not be.
Doug. You give him then advantage.
Ver. Not a whit.
Hot. Why say you so? Looks he not for supply?
Ver. So do we.
Hot. His is certain, ours is doubtful. 4
Wor. Good cousin, be advis'd. Stir not to-night.
Ver. Do not, my lord.
Doug. You do not counsel well.
You speak it out of fear, and cold heart.

Ver. Do me no slander, Douglas. By my life— 8
And I dare well maintain it with my life—
If well-respected honor bid me on,
I hold as little counsel with weak fear

77 stay: *linger*
10 well-respected: *well-considered, reasonable*

Act IV, Scene 3

As you, my lord, or any Scot that this day lives. 12
Let it be seen to-morrow in the battle
Which of us fears.
   Doug.   Yea, or to-night.
   Ver.   Content.
   Hot. To-night, say I.
   Ver. Come, come, it may not be. I wonder much, 16
Being men of such great leading as you are,
That you foresee not what impediments
Drag back our expedition. Certain horse
Of my cousin Vernon's are not yet come up. 20
Your uncle Worcester's horses came but to-day,
And now their pride and mettle is asleep,
Their courage with hard labor tame and dull,
That not a horse is half the half himself. 24
   Hot. So are the horses of the enemy
In general journey-bated and brought low.
The better part of ours are full of rest.
   Wor. The number of the king exceedeth ours. 28
For God's sake, cousin, stay till all come in.
                  The trumpet sounds a parley.

Enter Sir Walter Blunt.

   Blunt. I come with gracious offers from the king,
If you vouchsafe me hearing, and respect.
   Hot. Welcome, Sir Walter Blunt! and would to God
You were of our determination. 33
Some of us love you well, and even those some
Envy your great deservings and good name,

---

17 leading: *generalship*   24 half himself; *cf. n.*
26 journey-bated: *wearied with travel*
31 respect: *deference as the king's spokesman*

Because you are not of our quality, 36
But stand against us like an enemy.
   Blunt. And God defend but still I should stand so,
So long as out of limit and true rule
You stand against anointed majesty. 40
But to my charge. The king hath sent to know
The nature of your griefs, and whereupon
You conjure from the breast of civil peace
Such bold hostility, teaching his duteous land 44
Audacious cruelty. If that the king
Have any way your good deserts forgot,
Which he confesseth to be manifold,
He bids you name your griefs, and with all speed 48
You shall have your desires with interest,
And pardon absolute for yourself, and these
Herein misled by your suggestion.
   Hot. The king is kind, and well we know the king 52
Knows at what time to promise, when to pay.
My father, and my uncle, and myself,
Did give him that same royalty he wears.
And when he was not six and twenty strong, 56
Sick in the world's regard, wretched and low,
A poor unminded outlaw sneaking home,
My father gave him welcome to the shore.
And when he heard him swear and vow to God, 60
He came but to be Duke of Lancaster,
To sue his livery, and beg his peace
With tears of innocency, and terms of zeal,
My father, in kind heart and pity mov'd, 64

36 quality: *profession, party*   38 defend: *forbid*
51 suggestion: *instigation*
62 sue his livery: *bring suit for the delivery of his lands*

Act IV, Scene 3

Swore him assistance, and perform'd it too.
Now when the lords and barons of the realm
Perceiv'd Northumberland did lean to him,
The more and less came in with cap and knee, 68
Met him in boroughs, cities, villages,
Attended him on bridges, stood in lanes,
Laid gifts before him, proffer'd him their oaths,
Gave him their heirs as pages, follow'd him, 72
Even at the heels, in golden multitudes.
He presently, as greatness knows itself,
Steps me a little higher than his vow
Made to my father while his blood was poor 76
Upon the naked shore at Ravenspurgh,
And now, forsooth, takes on him to reform
Some certain edicts, and some strait decrees,
That lie too heavy on the commonwealth, 80
Cries out upon abuses, seems to weep
Over his country's wrongs, and by this face,
This seeming brow of justice, did he win
The hearts of all that he did angle for: 84
Proceeded further, cut me off the heads
Of all the favorites that the absent king
In deputation left behind him here,
When he was personal in the Irish war. 88
  Blunt. Tut! I came not to hear this.
  Hot.   Then to the point.
In short time after, he depos'd the king,
Soon after that depriv'd him of his life,
And in the neck of that task'd the whole state, 92

---

68 more and less: *great and small*   70 Attended: *awaited*
79 strait: *strict*   88 personal: *in person*
92 in the neck: *'on the heels'*   task'd: *taxed*

110 The First Part of Henry the Fourth

To make that worse, suffer'd his kinsman March
(Who is, if every owner were well plac'd,
Indeed his king) to be engag'd in Wales,
There without ransom to lie forfeited, 96
Disgrac'd me in my happy victories,
Sought to entrap me by intelligence,
Rated mine uncle from the council-board,
In rage dismiss'd my father from the court, 100
Broke oath on oath, committed wrong on wrong,
And in conclusion drove us to seek out
This head of safety, and withal to pry
Into his title, the which we find 104
Too indirect for long continuance.
    Blunt. Shall I return this answer to the king?
    Hot. Not so, Sir Walter. We'll withdraw awhile.
Go to the king, and let there be impawn'd 108
Some surety for a safe return again,
And in the morning early shall mine uncle
Bring him our purposes. And so farewell.
    Blunt. I would you would accept of grace and love.
    Hot. And may be so we shall.
    Blunt.   Pray God you do. 113
                                               Exeunt.

95 engag'd: *held as hostage*
98 intelligence: *information obtained through spies*
99 rated: *drove away by chiding*
103 head of safety: *army for protection*
105 indirect: *crooked*

Act IV, Scene 4

SCENE FOURTH

[York. The Archbishop's Palace]

Enter the Archbishop of York and Sir Michael.

Arch. Hie, good Sir Michael, bear this sealed brief
With winged haste to the lord marshal,
This to my cousin Scroop, and all the rest
To whom they are directed. If you knew 4
How much they do import, you would make haste.
  Sir M. My good lord,
I guess their tenor.
  Arch. Like enough you do.
To-morrow, good Sir Michael, is a day, 8
Wherein the fortune of ten thousand men
Must bide the touch. For sir, at Shrewsbury,
As I am truly given to understand,
The king with mighty and quick-raised power 12
Meets with Lord Harry. And I fear, Sir Michael,
What with the sickness of Northumberland,
Whose power was in the first proportion,
And what with Owen Glendower's absence thence, 16
Who with them was a rated sinew too—
And comes not in, o'er-rul'd by prophecies—
I fear the power of Percy is too weak
To wage an instant trial with the king. 20
  Sir M. Why my good lord, you need not fear. There is
Douglas, and Lord Mortimer.

---

1 brief: *letter*   10 bide the touch: *be put to the test*
17 rated sinew: *strength on which they counted*

112 The First Part of Henry the Fourth

Arch. No, Mortimer is not there.

Sir M. But there is Mordake, Vernon, Lord Harry
   Percy, 24
And there is my Lord of Worcester, and a head
Of gallant warriors, noble gentlemen.

Arch. And so there is. But yet the king hath drawn
The special head of all the land together: 28
The Prince of Wales, Lord John of Lancaster,
The noble Westmorland, and warlike Blunt,
And many mo corrivals and dear men
Of estimation and command in arms. 32

Sir M. Doubt not, my lord, they shall be well oppos'd.

Arch. I hope no less; yet needful 'tis to fear.
And to prevent the worst, Sir Michael, speed.
For if Lord Percy thrive not, ere the king 36
Dismiss his power, he means to visit us,
For he hath heard of our confederacy,
And 'tis but wisdom to make strong against him.
Therefore make haste. I must go write again 40
To other friends, and so farewell, Sir Michael. *Exeunt.*

31 mo: *more*   dear: *valued*
32 estimation: *reputation*

ACT FIFTH

SCENE FIRST

[Shrewsbury. The King's Camp]

*Enter the King, Prince of Wales, Lord John of Lancaster,
Sir Walter Blunt, and Falstaff.*

King. How bloodily the sun begins to peer
Above yon busky hill! The day looks pale
At his distemperature.
   Prince.   The southern wind
Doth play the trumpet to his purposes,   4
And by his hollow whistling in the leaves
Foretells a tempest and a blustering day.
   King. Then with the losers let it sympathize,
For nothing can seem foul to those that win.   8
                              The trumpet sounds.

Enter Worcester [and Vernon].

How now, my Lord of Worcester? 'Tis not well,
That you and I should meet upon such terms
As now we meet. You have deceiv'd our trust,
And made us doff our easy robes of peace,   12
To crush our old limbs in ungentle steel.
This is not well, my lord, this is not well.

Scene First. S. d.; *cf. n.*   2 busky: *bushy*
3 his distemperature: *the sun's inclemency*
4 his purposes: *'that which the sun portends' (Johnson)*
13 old limbs; *cf. n.*

114 The First Part of Henry the Fourth

What say you to it? Will you again unknit
This churlish knot of all-abhorred war, 16
And move in that obedient orb again,
Where you did give a fair and natural light,
And be no more an éxhal'd meteor,
A prodigy of fear, and a portent 20
Of broached mischief to the unborn times?
  Wor. Hear me, my liege.
For mine own part I could be well content,
To entertain the lag-end of my life 24
With quiet hours. For I do protest
I have not sought the day of this dislike.
  King. You have not sought it! How comes it then?
  Fal. Rebellion lay in his way, and he found it. 28
  Prince. Peace, chewet, peace!
  Wor. It pleas'd your majesty to turn your looks
Of favor from myself, and all our house,
And yet I must remember you, my lord, 32
We were the first and dearest of your friends.
For you my staff of office did I break
In Richard's time, and posted day and night
To meet you on the way, and kiss your hand, 36
When yet you were in place and in account
Nothing so strong and fortunate as I.
It was myself, my brother and his son,
That brought you home, and boldly did outdare 40
The dangers of the time. You swore to us,
And you did swear that oath at Doncaster,

---

17 obedient orb: *sphere of obedience*
19 éxhal'd: *drawn forth; especially vapors drawn forth by the sun and producing meteors*
21 broached: *begun* 29 chewet: *jackdaw* (?)

Act V, Scene 1

That you did nothing purpose 'gainst the state,
Nor claim no further than your new-fall'n right, 44
The seat of Gaunt, dukedom of Lancaster.
To this we swore our aid: but in short space
It rain'd down fortune show'ring on your head,
And such a flood of greatness fell on you, 48
What with our help, what with the absent king,
What with the injuries of a wanton time,
The seeming sufferances that you had borne,
And the contrarious winds that held the king 52
So long in his unlucky Irish wars,
That all in England did repute him dead—
And from this swarm of fair advantages,
You took occasion to be quickly woo'd 56
To gripe the general sway into your hand,
Forgot your oath to us at Doncaster,
And being fed by us, you us'd us so
As that ungentle gull, the cuckoo's bird, 60
Useth the sparrow: did oppress our nest,
Grew by our feeding to so great a bulk,
That even our love durst not come near your sight,
For fear of swallowing: but with nimble wing 64
We were enforc'd for safety's sake to fly
Out of your sight, and raise this present head,
Whereby we stand opposed by such means
As you yourself have forg'd against yourself 68
By unkind usage, dangerous countenance,
And violation of all faith and troth,
Sworn to us in your younger enterprise.

50 wanton time: *frivolous reign*   51 sufferances: *sufferings*
60 gull: *an unfledged nestling; cf. n.*
69 dangerous: *threatening*

King. These things, indeed, you have articulate, 72
Proclaim'd at market-crosses, read in churches,
To face the garment of rebellion
With some fine color that may please the eye
Of fickle changelings and poor discontents, 76
Which gape and rub the elbow at the news
Of hurlyburly innovation.
And never yet did insurrection want
Such water-colors to impaint his cause, 80
Nor moody beggars, starving for a time
Of pell-mell havoc and confusion.
  Prince. In both your armies there is many a soul
Shall pay full dearly for this encounter, 84
If once they join in trial. Tell your nephew,
The Prince of Wales doth join with all the world
In praise of Henry Percy. By my hopes,
This present enterprise set off his head, 88
I do not think a braver gentleman,
More active-valiant, or more valiant-young,
More daring, or more bold, is now alive
To grace this latter age with noble deeds. 92
For my part, I may speak it to my shame,
I have a truant been to chivalry,
And so I hear he doth account me too.
Yet this before my father's majesty— 96
I am content that he shall take the odds
Of his great name and estimation,
And will, to save the blood on either side,

72 articulate: *set forth in articles*   74 face: *trim*
76 discontents: *malcontents*   78 innovation: *revolution*
80 water-colors: *temporary dyes (pretexts)*
82 pell-mell havoc: *indiscriminate plunder*
88 set off his head: *taken from his account*

Act V, Scene 1 117

Try fortune with him in a single fight. 100
 King. And Prince of Wales, so dare we venture thee,
Albeit, considerations infinite
Do make against it. No, good Worcester, no.
We love our people well, even those we love 104
That are misled upon your cousin's part.
And, will they take the offer of our grace,
Both he, and they, and you, yea every man
Shall be my friend again, and I'll be his. 108
So tell your cousin, and bring me word
What he will do. But if he will not yield,
Rebuke and dread correction wait on us,
And they shall do their office. So be gone. 112
We will not now be troubled with reply.
We offer fair, take it advisedly.
      Exit Worcester [with Vernon].
 Prince. It will not be accepted, on my life.
The Douglas and the Hotspur both together 116
Are confident against the world in arms.
 King. Hence, therefore, every leader to his charge,
For on their answer will we set on them,
And God befriend us as our cause is just! 120
    Exeunt. Manent Prince and Falstaff.
 Fal. Hal, if thou see me down in the battle, and
bestride me, so; 'tis a point of friendship.
 Prince. Nothing but a colossus can do thee that
friendship. Say thy prayers, and farewell.
 Fal. I would it were bedtime, Hal, and all well.

101 dare we: *we would dare (in other circumstances)*
111 wait on us: *are in our service*
115 It: *i.e., the king's 'offer of grace' (line 106)*
120 S. d. Manent: *remain on the stage*
122 bestride: *stand over*   so: *very well*

118 The First Part of Henry the Fourth

Prince. Why, thou owest God a death. 126

Fal. 'Tis not due yet. I would be loath to pay him before his day. What need I be so forward with him that calls not on me? [*Exit Prince.*] Well, 'tis no matter. Honor pricks me on. Yea, but how if honor prick me off when I come on? how then? Can honor set to a leg? No. Or an arm? No. Or take away the grief of a wound? No. Honor hath no skill in surgery then? No. What is honor? A word. What is that word honor? Air. A trim reckoning! Who hath it? He that died o' Wednesday. Doth he feel it? No. Doth he hear it? No. 'Tis insensible then? Yea, to the dead. But will it not live with the living? No. Why? Detraction will not suffer it. Therefore I'll none of it. Honor is a mere scutcheon, and so ends my catechism. *Exit.* 141

SCENE SECOND

[*Shrewsbury. The Rebel Camp*]

Enter Worcester and Sir Richard Vernon.

Wor. O no, my nephew must not know, Sir Richard,
The liberal and kind offer of the king.

Ver. 'Twere best he did.

Wor.   Then are we all undone.
It is not possible, it cannot be   4
The king should keep his word in loving us.
He will suspect us still, and find a time

126, 127 *Cf. n.*
140 scutcheon: *shield with armorial bearings, carried in funeral processions*

Act V, Scene 2

To punish this offence in other faults.
Suspicion all our lives shall be stuck full of eyes,   8
For treason is but trusted like the fox,
Who, never so tame, so cherish'd and lock'd up,
Will have a wild trick of his ancestors.
Look how we can, or sad or merrily,   12
Interpretation will misquote our looks,
And we shall feed like oxen at a stall,
The better cherish'd still the nearer death.
My nephew's trespass may be well forgot—   16
It hath the excuse of youth and heat of blood,
And an adopted name of privilege—
A hare-brain'd Hotspur, govern'd by a spleen.
All his offences live upon my head   20
And on his father's. We did train him on,
And his corruption being ta'en from us,
We as the spring of all shall pay for all.
Therefore, good cousin, let not Harry know   24
In any case the offer of the king.
   Ver. Deliver what you will, I'll say 'tis so.
Here comes your cousin.

Enter Hotspur [and Douglas].

   Hot. My uncle is return'd. Deliver up   28
My Lord of Westmorland. Uncle, what news?
   Wor. The king will bid you battle presently.
   Doug. Defy him by the Lord of Westmorland.
   Hot. Lord Douglas, go you and tell him so.   32

---

8 Suspicion; *cf. n.*   12 or . . . or: *either . . . or*
18 adopted name of privilege: *nickname which carries certain privileges with it*
26 Deliver: *report*   28 Deliver up: *release*

120   The First Part of Henry the Fourth

Doug. Marry and shall, and very willingly!
Exit Douglas.

Wor. There is no seeming mercy in the king.

Hot. Did you beg any? God forbid!

Wor. I told him gently of our grievances, 36
Of his oath-breaking, which he mended thus,
By now forswearing that he is forsworn.
He calls us rebels, traitors, and will scourge
With haughty arms this hateful name in us. 40

Enter Douglas.

Doug. Arm, gentlemen! To arms! for I have thrown
A brave defiance in King Henry's teeth,
And Westmorland, that was engag'd, did bear it,
Which cannot choose but bring him quickly on. 44

Wor. The Prince of Wales stepp'd forth before the king,
And, nephew, challeng'd you to single fight.

Hot. O would the quarrel lay upon our heads,
And that no man might draw short breath to-day 48
But I and Harry Monmouth! Tell me, tell me,
How show'd his tasking? seem'd it in contempt?

Ver. No, by my soul, I never in my life
Did hear a challenge urg'd more modestly, 52
Unless a brother should a brother dare
To gentle exercise and proof of arms.
He gave you all the duties of a man,
Trimm'd up your praises with a princely tongue, 56
Spoke your deservings like a chronicle,

---

38 forswearing: *denying on oath*   forsworn: *perjured*
50 tasking: *challenge*
55 all the duties of a man: *all that one man owes another*

Act V, Scene 2 121

Making you ever better than his praise,
By still dispraising praise valu'd with you:
And, which became him like a prince indeed, 60
He made a blushing cital of himself,
And chid his truant youth with such a grace
As if he master'd there a double spirit
Of teaching and of learning instantly. 64
There did he pause. But let me tell the world,
If he outlive the envy of this day,
England did never owe so sweet a hope,
So much miscónstru'd in his wantonness. 68

Hot. Cousin, I think thou art enamored
On his follies. Never did I hear
Of any prince so wild a libertine.
But be he as he will, yet once ere night 72
I will embrace him with a soldier's arm,
That he shall shrink under my courtesy.
Arm, arm with speed! And fellows, soldiers, friends,
Better consider what you have to do, 76
Than I, that have not well the gift of tongue,
Can lift your blood up with persuasion.

Enter a Messenger.

Mess. My lord, here are letters for you.
Hot. I cannot read them now. 80
O gentlemen, the time of life is short.
To spend that shortness basely were too long,
If life did ride upon a dial's point,
Still ending at the arrival of an hour. 84
And if we live, we live to tread on kings,

61 cital of: *reference to*   67 owe: *own*
71 libertine; *cf. n.*   83 dial's point: *hand of a clock*

If die, brave death, when princes die with us!
Now, for our consciences, the arms are fair
When the intent of bearing them is just. 88

Enter another Messenger.

Mess. My lord, prepare! The king comes on apace.
Hot. I thank him that he cuts me from my tale,
For I profess not talking. Only this—
Let each man do his best. And here draw I 92
A sword, whose temper I intend to stain
With the best blood that I can meet withal
In the adventure of this perilous day.
Now, *Esperance!* Percy! and set on. 96
Sound all the lofty instruments of war,
And by that music let us all embrace,
For, heaven to earth, some of us never shall
A second time do such a courtesy. 100

Here they embrace. The trumpets sound. The King enters with his power. Alarm to the battle. Then enter Douglas and Sir Walter Blunt.

Blunt. What is thy name, that in battle thus
Thou crossest me? What honor dost thou seek
Upon my head?
Doug. Know then, my name is Douglas,
And I do haunt thee in the battle thus 104
Because some tell me that thou art a king.
Blunt. They tell thee true.
Doug. The Lord of Stafford dear to-day hath bought
Thy likeness, for instead of thee, King Harry, 108
This sword hath ended him. So shall it thee

100 S. d.; *cf. n.*   101 *Cf. n.*

Act V, Scene 2

Unless thou yield thee as my prisoner.

  Blunt. I was not born a yielder, thou proud Scot,
And thou shalt find a king that will revenge   112
Lord Stafford's death.

              They fight. Douglas kills Blunt.

        Then enter Hotspur.

  Hot. O Douglas, hadst thou fought at Holmedon thus
I never had triúmph'd upon a Scot.

  Doug. All's done, all's won! Here breathless lies the
    king.   116

  Hot. Where?

  Doug. Here.

  Hot. This, Douglas? No. I know this face full well.
A gallant knight he was—his name was Blunt—   120
Semblably furnish'd like the king himself.

  Doug. Ah, 'fool' go with thy soul whither it goes!
A borrow'd title hast thou bought too dear.
Why didst thou tell me that thou wert a king?   124

  Hot. The king hath many marching in his coats.

  Doug. Now by my sword, I will kill all his coats.
I'll murder all his wardrobe, piece by piece,
Until I meet the king.

  Hot.   Up, and away!   128
Our soldiers stand full fairly for the day.   *Exeunt.*

      Alarm. Enter Falstaff solus.

  Fal. Though I could 'scape shot-free at London, I
fear the shot here. Here's no scoring but upon the
pate. Soft! who are you? Sir Walter Blunt! There's

---

120 Cf. *n.*   121 Semblably furnish'd: *dressed to resemble*
122 'fool' go with thy soul; cf. *n.*
130 shot-free: *without having to pay*

124   The First Part of Henry the Fourth

honor for you. Here's no vanity! I am as hot as molten lead, and as heavy too. God keep lead out of me! I need no more weight than mine own bowels. I have led my ragamuffins where they are peppered. There's not three of my hundred and fifty left alive, and they are for the town's end, to beg during life. But who comes here? 139

Enter the Prince.

Prince. What, stand'st thou idle here? Lend me thy sword. 140
Many a nobleman lies stark and stiff
Under the hoofs of vaunting enemies,
Whose deaths are yet unreveng'd. I prithee lend me thy sword. 143

Fal. O Hal, I prithee give me leave to breathe awhile. Turk Gregory never did such deeds in arms as I have done this day. I have paid Percy, I have made him sure.

Prince. He is indeed, and living to kill thee. I prithee lend me thy sword. 149

Fal. Nay, before God, Hal, if Percy be alive thou gett'st not my sword, but take my pistol if thou wilt.

Prince. Give it me. What? Is it in the case? 152

Fal. Ay, Hal, 'tis hot, 'tis hot. There's that will sack a city.

The Prince draws it out, and finds it to be a bottle of sack.

Prince. What, is it a time to jest and dally now?
He throws the bottle at him. Exit.

Fal. Well, if Percy be alive, I'll pierce him. If he

145 Turk Gregory; *cf. n.*   156 pierce; *cf. n.*

Act V, Scene 2

do come in my way, so. If he do not, if I come in his willingly, let him make a carbonado of me. I like not such grinning honor as Sir Walter hath. Give me life! which if I can save, so: if not, honor comes unlooked for, and there's an end. *Exit.*

SCENE THIRD

[*Another Part of the Battle Field. The King's Post*]

Alarm. Excursions. Enter the King, the Prince, Lord John of Lancaster, Earl of Westmorland.

   King. I prithee, Harry, withdraw thyself. Thou bleedest too much. Lord John of Lancaster, go you with him.
   John. Not I, my lord, unless I did bleed too. 4
   Prince. I beseech your majesty make up,
Lest your retirement do amaze your friends.
   King. I will do so. My lord of Westmorland, lead him to his tent. 8
   West. Come, my lord, I'll lead you to your tent.
   Prince. Lead me, my lord? I do not need your help,
And God forbid a shallow scratch should drive
The Prince of Wales from such a field as this, 12
Where stain'd nobility lies trodden on,
And rebels' arms triúmph in massacres!
   John. We breathe too long. Come, Cousin Westmorland,
Our duty this way lies. For God's sake, come. 16
        [*Exeunt Lord John and Westmorland.*]

---

158 carbonado: *a piece of meat slashed for broiling*
5 make up: *go forward*   6 amaze: *alarm*

126 The First Part of Henry the Fourth

Prince. By God, thou hast deceiv'd me, Lancaster.
I did not think thee lord of such a spirit.
Before, I lov'd thee as a brother, John,
But now I do respect thee as my soul.   20
   King. I saw him hold Lord Percy at the point,
With lustier maintenance than I did look for
Of such an ungrown warrior.
   Prince.   O this boy
Lends mettle to us all.   *Exit.*

Enter Douglas.

   Doug. Another king? They grow like Hydra's heads. 25
I am the Douglas, fatal to all those
That wear those colors on them. What art thou
That counterfeit'st the person of a king?   28
   King. The king himself, who, Douglas, grieves at heart
So many of his shadows thou hast met
And not the very king. I have two boys
Seek Percy and thyself about the field,   32
But seeing thou fall'st on me so luckily
I will assay thee. So defend thyself.
   Doug. I fear thou art another counterfeit.
And yet, in faith, thou bear'st thee like a king.   36
But mine I am sure thou art whoe'er thou be,
And thus I win thee.

               They fight, the king being in danger,

               Enter Prince of Wales.

22 lustier maintenance: *more vigorous bearing*
25 Hydra: *a fabled monster, whose heads grew again as they were cut off*
32 Seek: *who seek*

Act V, Scene 3

Prince. Hold up thy head, vile Scot, or thou art like
Never to hold it up again! the spirits
Of valiant Shirley, Stafford, Blunt are in my arms.
It is the Prince of Wales that threatens thee,
Who never promiseth but he means to pay.
                        They fight. Douglas flieth.
Cheerly, my lord! How fares your Grace?
Sir Nicholas Gawsey hath for succor sent,
And so hath Clifton. I'll to Clifton straight.
   King. Stay and breathe awhile.
Thou hast redeem'd thy lost opinion,
And show'd thou mak'st some tender of my life,
In this fair rescue thou hast brought to me.
   Prince. O God! they did me too much injury,
That ever said I hearken'd for your death.
If it were so, I might have let alone
The insulting hand of Douglas over you,
Which would have been as speedy in your end
As all the poisonous potions in the world,
And sav'd the treacherous labor of your son.
   King. Make up to Clifton. I'll to Sir Nicholas Gawsey.
                                                Exit.

Enter Hotspur.

Hot. If I mistake not, thou art Harry Monmouth.
Prince. Thou speak'st as if I would deny my name.
Hot. My name is Harry Percy.
Prince.   Why then I see
A very valiant rebel of the name.
I am the Prince of Wales, and think not, Percy,
To share with me in glory any more.

43 but: *unless*   49 mak'st some tender: *hast some regard for*
52 hearken'd for: *watched for, desired*

128   The First Part of Henry the Fourth

Two stars keep not their motion in one sphere,
Nor can one England brook a double reign
Of Harry Percy and the Prince of Wales.
   Hot. Nor shall it, Harry, for the hour is come   68
To end the one of us, and would to God
Thy name in arms were now as great as mine.
   Prince. I'll make it greater ere I part from thee,
And all the budding honors on thy crest   72
I'll crop to make a garland for my head.
   Hot. I can no longer brook thy vanities.   *They fight.*

   Enter Falstaff.

   Fal. Well said, Hal! to it, Hal! Nay, you shall find
no boy's play here, I can tell you.   76
      *Enter Douglas. He fighteth with Falstaff. He
      [i.e., Falstaff] falls down as if he were dead.
      [Exit Douglas.] The Prince killeth Percy.*
   Hot. O Harry, thou hast robb'd me of my youth.
I better brook the loss of brittle life
Than those proud titles thou hast won of me.
They wound my thoughts worse than thy sword my
      flesh.   80
But thoughts (the slaves of life) and life (time's fool)
And time, that takes survey of all the world,
Must have a stop. O, I could prophesy,
But that the earthy and cold hand of death   84
Lies on my tongue. No, Percy, thou art dust,
And food for—   *[Dies.]*
   Prince. For worms, brave Percy. Fare thee well, great
      heart!

65 Cf. n.   75 Well said: *well tried, well done*
80 They: *i.e., the titles lost*

Act V, Scene 3   129

Ill-weav'd ambition, how much art thou shrunk!   88
When that this body did contain a spirit,
A kingdom for it was too small a bound,
But now two paces of the vilest earth
Is room enough. This earth, that bears thee dead,   92
Bears not alive so stout a gentleman.
If thou wert sensible of courtesy,
I should not make so dear a show of zeal.
But let my favors hide thy mangled face,   96
And even in thy behalf I'll thank myself,
For doing these fair rites of tenderness.
Adieu, and take thy praise with thee to heaven!
Thy ignominy sleep with thee in the grave,   100
But not remember'd in thy epitaph!
                 He spieth Falstaff on the ground.
What, old acquaintance! Could not all this flesh
Keep in a little life? Poor Jack, farewell!
I could have better spar'd a better man.   104
O I should have a heavy miss of thee,
If I were much in love with vanity.
Death hath not struck so fat a deer to-day,
Though many dearer, in this bloody fray.   108
Embowell'd will I see thee by and by.
Till then in blood by noble Percy lie.   *Exit.*

            Falstaff riseth up.

Fal. Embowelled? if thou embowel me to-day, I'll give you leave to powder me and eat me too to-

---

93 stout: *valiant*   95 dear: *affectionate*
96 favors; *cf. n.*
109 Embowell'd: *disembowelled for embalming*
112 powder: *salt*

morrow. 'Sblood! 'twas time to counterfeit, or that hot termagant Scot had paid me scot and lot too. Counterfeit? I lie, I am no counterfeit. To die is to be a counterfeit, for he is but the counterfeit of a man, who hath not the life of a man: but to counterfeit dying, when a man thereby liveth, is to be no counterfeit, but the true and perfect image of life indeed. The better part of valor is discretion, in the which better part I have saved my life. 'Zounds! I am afraid of this gunpowder Percy, though he be dead. How if he should counterfeit too and rise? By my faith, I am afraid he would prove the better counterfeit. Therefore I'll make him sure: yea, and I'll swear I killed him. Why may not he rise as well as I? Nothing confutes me but eyes, and nobody sees me. Therefore, sirrah, with a new wound in your thigh, come you along with me. 129

He takes up Hotspur on his back.

Enter Prince and John of Lancaster.

Prince. Come, brother John, full bravely hast thou flesh'd
Thy maiden sword.
    John.   But soft! Whom have we here?
Did you not tell me this fat man was dead? 132
  Prince. I did. I saw him dead, breathless and bleeding
On the ground.—Art thou alive? or is it
Fantasy that plays upon our eyesight?
I prithee speak. We will not trust our eyes 136
Without our ears. Thou art not what thou seem'st.

114 termagant: *violent; cf. n.*   scot and lot: *a tax paid according to one's ability and resources*

Act V, Scene 3

Fal. No, that's certain. I am not a double man: but if I be not Jack Falstaff, then am I a Jack. There is Percy [*throwing down the body*]. If your father will do me any honor, so: if not, let him kill the next Percy himself. I look to be either earl or duke, I can assure you.

Prince. Why, Percy I killed myself, and saw thee dead. 144

Fal. Didst thou? Lord, Lord, how this world is given to lying! I grant you I was down, and out of breath, and so was he, but we rose both at an instant, and fought a long hour by Shrewsbury clock. If I may be believed, so: if not, let them that should reward valor bear the sin upon their own heads. I'll take it upon my death, I gave him this wound in the thigh. If the man were alive, and would deny it, 'zounds, I would make him eat a piece of my sword.

John. This is the strangest tale that ever I heard.

Prince. This is the strangest fellow, brother John. Come, bring your luggage nobly on your back. 156
For my part, if a lie may do thee grace,
I'll gild it with the happiest terms I have.

A retreat is sounded.

The trumpet sounds retreat, the day is ours.
Come brother, let us to the highest of the field, 160
To see what friends are living, who are dead. *Exeunt.*

Fal. I'll follow, as they say, for reward. He that rewards me, God reward him! If I do grow great, I'll grow less, for I'll purge and leave sack, and live cleanly as a nobleman should do. *Exit.*

160 highest: *highest ground, best viewpoint; cf. n.*
162 I'll follow; *cf. n.*

SCENE FOURTH

[*The Battle Field*]

The trumpets sound. Enter the King, Prince of Wales, Lord John of Lancaster, Earl of Westmorland, with Worcester and Vernon prisoners.

King. Thus ever did rebellion find rebuke.
Ill-spirited Worcester, did not we send grace,
Pardon, and terms of love to all of you?
And wouldst thou turn our offers contrary? 4
Misuse the tenor of thy kinsman's trust?
Three knights upon our party slain to-day,
A noble earl, and many a creature else,
Had been alive this hour, 8
If like a Christian thou hadst truly borne
Betwixt our armies true intelligence.

Wor. What I have done my safety urg'd me to:
And I embrace this fortune patiently, 12
Since not to be avoided it falls on me.

King. Bear Worcester to the death and Vernon too.
Other offenders we will pause upon.
                  Exit Worcester and Vernon [*guarded*].
How goes the field? 16

Prince. The noble Scot, Lord Douglas, when he saw
The fortune of the day quite turn'd from him,
The noble Percy slain, and all his men
Upon the foot of fear, fled with the rest, 20
And falling from a hill, he was so bruis'd

20 Upon the foot of fear: *flying in fear*

Act V, Scene 4

That the pursuers took him. At my tent
The Douglas is, and I beseech your Grace
I may dispose of him.
  King.   With all my heart.
  Prince. Then, brother John of Lancaster, to you
This honorable bounty shall belong.
Go to the Douglas, and deliver him
Up to his pleasure, ransomless and free.
His valors shown upon our crests to-day
Have taught us how to cherish such high deeds,
Even in the bosom of our adversaries.
  John. I thank your Grace for this high courtesy,
Which I shall give away immediately.
  King. Then this remains, that we divide our power.
You, son John, and my cousin Westmorland
Towards York shall bend you, with your dearest speed,
To meet Northumberland and the prelate Scroop,
Who, as we hear, are busily in arms.
Myself and you, son Harry, will towards Wales,
To fight with Glendower and the Earl of March.
Rebellion in this land shall loose his sway,
Meeting the check of such another day,
And since this business so fair is done,
Let us not leave till all our own be won.   *Exeunt.*

29 valors: *acts of prowess*   36 dearest: *best*
44 leave: *leave off*

FINIS

NOTES

Aᴛ *the time of his sudden death in June of 1946, Professor Brooke had completed his work on the text, notes, and glosses for* Hamlet, King Lear, Othello, *and* I Henry IV. *The editorial tasks which he left unfinished—preparation of some of the final copy for the press, reading of the proofs, compilation of the* Indexes of Words Glossed, *decisions as to certain matters of style and format, and, in the case of* I Henry IV, *the rescuing of the text from the prescriptive punctuation of the eighteenth-century editors—have been undertaken by Professor Benjamin Nangle.*

TEXTUAL NOTE. The differences between the Quarto text of this play, first printed in 1598, and the Folio text published in 1623 are unusually small. The Folio here has little or no independent authority. It appears to have been set up from a copy of the Quarto of 1613 (the fifth in sequence from the *editio princeps* of 1598) and it passed on, with additions of its own, the great body of small textual errors which this popular play had picked up in the course of rapid quarto printing. Even in the matter of stage directions the Folio has little new to offer; it usually reprints the quarto directions with only casual changes of wording. It did, however, divide the play into acts and scenes, something not attempted in the quartos, and did this with completeness and accuracy. In the present edition no changes have been made in the Folio act and scene headings except to translate them out of their Latin style: 'Actus Primus. Scaena Prima.,' *etc.* The stage directions reproduce usually those of the 1598 Quarto, sometimes those of the Folio. Necessary amplifications and other essential matter omitted in the original editions are supplied within square brackets.

The present text is based mainly on that of the extant 1598 edition, usually referred to as the First Quarto.

There was, however, an earlier edition, probably printed a few months before, of which one single sheet of four leaves is preserved in the Folger Shakespeare Library. It enables us to recover a word that Shakespeare almost certainly wrote, the word *fat* in II.ii.110.

In Shakespeare's usage it was optional to give full syllabic value to the ending *-ed* of past verbal forms or (as is generally done now) to contract this ending with the preceding syllable. In the present text final *-ed* must always be pronounced as a separate syllable in order to preserve the original rhythm of the verse. Where rhythm requires the contracted form, the spelling *-'d* is used.

Shakespeare accented a number of words on syllables which do not now bear the accent, and sometimes his practice in this matter was inconsistent. Where an unusual accentuation is required, it is indicated by an acute mark over the stressed vowel, as in *éxact*.

Obsolete words and words employed in now unusual senses are explained in footnotes the first time they occur in the text. Repetitions are not noted and when they occur can be found in the *Index of Words Glossed* at the end of the volume.

The critical and general notes in the present section are announced by the symbol, *cf. n.*, at the bottom of the page of text to which each has relevance. A name at the end of a note (in parentheses) indicates the authority; but no special effort is made to give credit for material which is common property or which is, so far as known, new in the present edition.

I.i.4. *stronds afar remote.* The idea of pilgrimage reminds Shakespeare of the opening of Chaucer's *Canterbury Tales,* with its allusion to palmers seeking 'straunge strondes.'

136   The First Part of Henry the Fourth

I.i.5. *entrance of this soil.* The earth is personified, and the dry surface is called her mouth.

I.i.26. *fourteen hundred years ago.* The purpose is to give the audience the historical date, which was 1402. The figure, however, is about thirty years in error, because the Christian era is reckoned from Christ's birth, not his crucifixion.

I.i.28. Cf. the last lines of Shakespeare's *Richard II*, King Henry's speech when news is brought him that, at his suggestion, King Richard, his predecessor whose throne he has usurped, has been murdered:

> Lords, I protest, my soul is full of woe
> That blood should sprinkle me to make me grow:
> Come, mourn with me for that I do lament
> And put on sullen black incontinent:
> I'll make a journey to the Holy Land
> To wash this blood from off my guilty hand.

During the year (actually two and a half years) which has intervened, civil wars have prevented the fulfilment of this vow.

I.i.38. *Mortimer.* Earl of March, rightful heir to the throne of England (see genealogical table in note on I.iii.145,146), now (according to the play) in command of King Henry's forces on the western front.

I.i.52. *Holy-rood day.* Holy Cross Day, 14 September.

I.i.53. *Young Harry Percy.* The youngest member of the great Percy family, now in command of the king's forces on the northern front. The Percies (see The Actors' Names) had been King Henry's chief supporters in his usurpation of the throne.

I.i.57,58. *As . . . the news was told.* As we learned by the sound of their artillery and by probable conjecture.

I.i.71. *Mordake* (i.e. Murdoch Stuart), *Earl of Fife.* He was not son to beaten Douglas, but to the Duke of Albany, regent of Scotland. Shakespeare's error is due to a mistake in punctuation in Holinshed's list of Hotspur's prisoners, which reads: 'Mordacke earle of Fife, son to the governour Archembald earle Dowglas,' etc. A comma was omitted after 'governour,' and Shakespeare understood that 'Archembald' was 'governour.'

I.i.91–95. By the law of arms, the king might claim only such prisoners as were of royal blood, and the historical Hotspur was therefore within his rights in refusing to send to the king any

Notes

prisoners except Mordake. But Shakespeare did not know that Mordake was of royal blood (see preceding note) and he was apparently ignorant of the law of arms which gave Hotspur the right to keep the rest of the prisoners. No attempt is made to explain why Shakespeare's Hotspur sent Mordake to the king—Shakespeare merely follows the facts as set down in Holinshed. The indignation of King Henry and Westmorland, in this scene, at 'young Percy's pride'; Hotspur's conciliatory tone and his explanations when he appears at court (I.iii.); and the fact that neither Hotspur nor his uncle, Worcester, the experienced diplomat, ever suggests that Hotspur has a legal right to his prisoners; all these things indicate that Shakespeare's Hotspur is not within his rights in keeping the prisoners. His refusal was, at first, a thoughtless and impetuous act; and the refusal once made, the shrewd Worcester saw reasons for influencing his nephew to stand by this first hasty reply to the king's demand.

I.i.97. *Malevolent to you in all aspects.* An astrological allusion, referring to the supposed good and evil influences of the planets. The king uses another astrological figure in his address to Worcester in V.i.17–21.

I.i.107. *uttered.* Used here in its peculiar Elizabethan sense, namely, to put into circulation or to offer to the public. The substance of the king's speech is: 'Dismiss the lords until Wednesday next, but you yourself return to me at once, for more is to be said and done, than I can say or do in public in my present angry condition.'

I.ii.S.d. *Enter Prince of Wales and Sir John Falstaff.* They do not come in together. Falstaff is asleep on a bench and the Prince is awaking him as the scene opens.

I.ii.14. *seven stars.* The Pleiades.

I.ii.15. *wandering knight.* El Donzel del Febo, Knight of the Sun (or Phœbus), hero of a popular Spanish romance. This quotation is perhaps from some contemporary ballad founded on the romance.

I.ii.17–30. Falstaff plays on the word Grace, using it first as a title, then in reference to the spiritual state of grace, and finally as 'grace before meat.' From this simple pun he proceeds to a more complicated play on words. There is the obvious play on *night* and *knight* in line 24, followed in lines 24,25 by the play on the words *body, beauty,* and *booty,* in each of which the vowel sound, in Shakespeare's day, approximated the round

138   The First Part of Henry the Fourth

o sound, as in *note*. Finally there is the play on the phrase *under whose countenance*.

I.ii.43,44. *buff jerkin . . . durance.* A buff jerkin, the jacket of heavy yellowish leather regularly worn by a sheriff's officer, is certainly durable and perhaps both confining in itself and a symbol of confinement (durance vile) for offenders; but the phrase *robe of durance* seems, when naturally interpreted, to introduce an illogical shift from the costume of the officer to that of his prisoner. Perhaps Hal's lack of logic is intentional, since if the hostess can be called a most sweet wench, all distinctions are lost.

I.ii.80. Eating the flesh of a hare was supposed to generate melancholy.

I.ii.81. *Moorditch.* A stagnant ditch and morass outside the north wall of London. The Theatre and Curtain playhouses were close by.

I.ii.93. *damnable iteration.* A damnable trick of quoting and misapplying. Falstaff and the Prince have both been parodying the first chapter of *Proverbs* (verse 20 ff.): 'Wisdom crieth without; she uttereth her voice in the streets. She crieth in the chief place of concourse . . . "I have stretched out my hand, and no man regarded; but ye have set at naught all my counsel, and would none of my reproof." '

I.ii.109. *Gadshill.* The *nom de guerre* of one of the robbers and the scene of his exploits.

I.ii.118,119. *a cup of Madeira and a cold capon's leg.* The keeping of Lent was strenuously demanded in the Anglican as well as the Catholic Church.

I.ii.128. *There are pilgrims going to Canterbury.* Perhaps another Chaucer allusion (cf. n. on I.i.4). The pilgrims are not again mentioned, and they are the only element in this part of the play that is not contemporary Elizabethan.

I.ii.133. *Eastcheap.* The district in central London where the Boar's Head Tavern, the rendezvous of Hal and Falstaff, was situated.

I.ii.144. *stand for ten shillings.* Primarily, take your stand as a highwayman for a profit of that amount; but Falstaff is also quibbling on the name of the gold coin, 'royal,' which stood for (had the value of) ten shillings.

I.ii.145. *Well, then*, etc. The Prince is teasing Falstaff. He has no idea of going, as line 148 shows.

Notes 139

I.ii.162. *the latter spring.* Good Elizabethan idiom. Pope emended it to 'thou latter spring.'

I.ii.162,163. *Allhallown summer.* The warm weather which comes at about the time of All Saints' Day, 1 November; called in America Indian Summer. The reference is to Falstaff's youthful spirit in his old age.

I.ii.166. *Bardolph, Peto.* In all the early texts these names are here replaced by 'Harvey, Rossill.' The characters were probably so called, when Falstaff was called 'Oldcastle,' and later given new names. (In the Quarto text Bardolph is regularly called 'Bardoll.')

I.ii.183. *sirrah.* The ordinary form of address to children and servants; here, a sign of Poins's undue familiarity with the Prince.

I.ii.189,190. *the third.* Falstaff. Shakespeare's inaccuracy in unimportant details is well illustrated here. He has just mentioned four robbers (line 166), and now implies, at least, that there are to be but three.

I.ii.201–223. One interpretation of the Prince's speech is that it is a striking example of the use of soliloquy in a choral function, to give the audience information uncolored by the personality of the speaker; and that Shakespeare is here describing the Prince's character and expects us to accept the description at face value without imputing vanity or insincerity to his mouthpiece, who has ceased to speak in his own person. See L. L. Schücking, *Character Problems in Shakespeare's Plays,* 1922, 217–221. Another school of critics sees in this speech the first indication of the cool and calculating nature of the Prince.

I.iii.S.d. *Windsor Castle.* The scene is stated by Holinshed. Cf.I.i. 104.

I.iii.36. *milliner.* In Shakespeare's time, milliners, i.e., dealers in women's clothes from Milan, were for the most part men.

I.iii.56. *God save the mark.* An expression of impatient scorn (O.E.D.).

I.iii.137. *Bolingbroke.* King Henry is referred to by several names during the course of the play. Before his accession he was commonly known as Henry of Bolingbroke, from the fact that he was born in Bolingbroke Castle in Lincolnshire. He also bore the titles Earl of Derby, Duke of Hereford, and, after his father's death, Duke of Lancaster.

I.iii.145,146. The following genealogical table will help to make clear this question of the succession to the English throne:

140 The First Part of Henry the Fourth

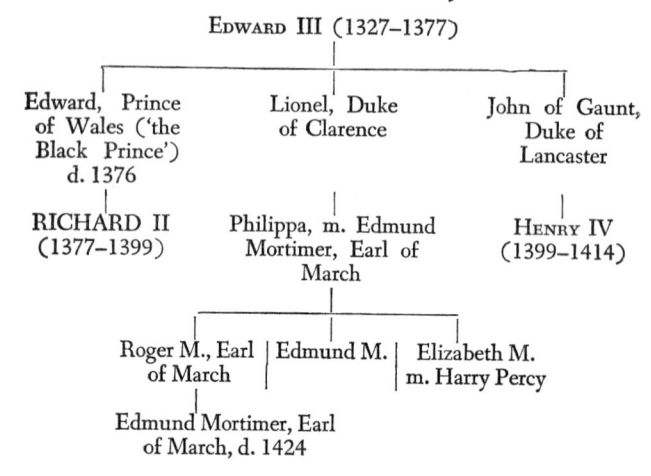

```
                        EDWARD III (1327-1377)
                                 |
    ┌────────────────────────────┼────────────────────────────┐
Edward, Prince              Lionel, Duke              John of Gaunt,
of Wales ('the              of Clarence                 Duke of
Black Prince')                   |                     Lancaster
d. 1376                          |                         |
    |                    Philippa, m. Edmund               |
RICHARD II               Mortimer, Earl of             HENRY IV
(1377-1399)                    March                  (1399-1414)
                                 |
                ┌────────────────┼────────────────┐
          Roger M., Earl   Edmund M.    Elizabeth M.
            of March                    m. Harry Percy
               |
         Edmund Mortimer, Earl
            of March, d. 1424
```

Shakespeare follows the chroniclers in confusing Edmund Mortimer, the son of Philippa, with Edmund Mortimer, the son of Roger. It was Roger Mortimer who was King Richard's heir, and was so proclaimed in the October Parliament of 1385. At his death in 1398, one year before King Richard's, his seven-year-old son succeeded to his claim. But it was the elder Edmund, brother to Roger, who fought Glendower and married his daughter. Hotspur's brother-in-law, therefore, was not heir to the throne. The heir, as the table shows, was the nephew of Lady Percy, and in III.i.196, Mortimer refers to Lady Percy as 'my aunt Percy.' Here (line 156), and in line 80, Mortimer is represented as Hotspur's brother-in-law.

I.iii.245. *York*. Edmund of Langley, Duke of York, younger brother to John of Gaunt, uncle to King Richard and King Henry. Richard had appointed York regent of England during the king's absence in Ireland. Richard had previously exiled Henry, and the latter chose this period of the king's absence from his realm to return and claim his father's estates, which had been unjustly confiscated by Richard to pay for this same Irish expedition. Henry was met at Ravenspurgh, on the coast of Yorkshire, by Northumberland; at Doncaster, in southern Yorkshire, by Worcester; and finally at Berkeley Castle, in

Notes

Gloucestershire, by Hotspur. The interview between Hotspur and Henry, from which Hotspur quotes in his next speech, is presented in Shakespeare's *Richard II*, II.iii.

I.iii.252. *Look when.* A remarkable localism, used frequently by Shakespeare in his earlier works. See Mark Eccles, 'Shakespeare's Use of *Look How* and similar Idioms' (*J.E.G.P.*, July, 1943).

I.iii.269. *the Lord Scroop.* The Earl of Wiltshire, one of the adherents of King Richard, executed by order of Henry; see *Richard II*, III.ii.141 ff. He was not the brother of the archbishop, as Holinshed states, but of an allied family.

II.i.S.d. *The Yard of a Carriers' Inn.* The carriers transported produce and other merchandise between London and the country, using the appointed inn-yards for loading and unloading. The companies of actors employed the same inn-yards for plays when regular playhouses were not available. The scene here presented is doubtless based on what Shakespeare would have observed at the Cross Keys Inn in London, where his company acted in 1594.

II.i.2. *Charles' Wain.* Probably a corruption of 'churl's wain' or 'countryman's wagon,' a name for the constellation now known as the Great Bear.

II.i.15. There is an old superstition, referred to in Pliny's *Natural History*, ix.47, that fishes are infested with fleas. Cf. line 21.

II.i.25. *Charing Cross.* In Shakespeare's time a village on the road from London to Westminster; now in the heart of Greater London.

II.i.33. *two o'clock.* Compare line 1 above. The carriers suspect Gadshill and refuse to co-operate (Steevens).

II.i.61. *Saint Nicholas.* A popular saint in the Roman and Russian Churches, now familiarly known as Santa Claus. He was the patron saint of scholars, children, parish clerks, travellers, sailors, and pawn-brokers. His aid was invoked by travellers to protect them from perils of the road, especially from robbers. But here the allusion is to his opposite, 'Old Nick,' the devil.

II.i.73 ff. *foot land-rakers*, foot-pads; *long-staff sixpenny strikers*, fellows who would knock a man down to get sixpence from him; *mustachio-purple-hued malt worms*, fellows whose moustaches are so constantly immersed in ale that they have become purple; *tranquillity*, people who live at ease; *great oneyers*, great ones (with a play on the words *one* and *own* which were pronounced alike); *such as can hold in*, such as can keep their own counsel (an accomplishment which Gadshill seems to find it difficult to imitate).

II.i.85. Greasing of boots to make them waterproof was called 'liquoring' them.

II.i.86,87. *receipt of fernseed.* The seeding of ferns was a mystery to early botanists. According to popular superstition, fernseed was visible only on Saint John's Eve (23 June), and those who gathered it then, according to a certain rite, were themselves rendered invisible.

II.i.95. *homo is a common name to all men.* Even a false thief is a true *homo.* A small joke out of Lily's Latin grammar.

II.ii.2. *frets like a gummed velvet.* Velvet stiffened with gum very soon chafed.

II.ii.43. *heir-apparent garters.* 'Alluding to the Order of the Garter, in which he was enrolled as heir-apparent' (Johnson).

II.ii.66. *John of Gaunt.* There is a pun, as if on 'John o' Gaunt' and 'John o' Paunch' (Kittredge).

II.iii.S.d. The writer of this letter is not specified.

II.iii.33. I could divide myself into two parts and then fight with myself.

II.iii.37. *Kate.* The actual name of Hotspur's wife was Elizabeth, not Kate; cf. genealogical table on page 140. Shakespeare seems to have had a peculiar fondness for the name Kate.

II.iii.46,47. Why have you allowed musing and melancholy, which have made you *thick-eyed,* i.e., blind to all outward things, to make you forget your attention to me, which is my *treasure?*

II.iii.54. The basilisk cannon was named from the fabulous monster whose look was reputed to kill. The culverin is also named from a serpent.

II.iii.94. *crowns.* Used quibblingly: broken heads, or damaged coin, still in circulation, 'passing current.' Behind this is the idea of the crown of the kingdom at which Hotspur means to have a crack.

II.iv.1. *fat room.* Certainly not 'vat-room,' as sometimes explained. It is the Prince, not Poins, who has been in the latter.

II.iv.19. *tinker.* Tinkers were famous for their capacity for strong drink and for their picturesque vocabulary.

II.iv.55. *Michaelmas.* The feast of St. Michael, 29 September; one of the four quarter days of the English business year.

II.iv.74 ff. Hal here talks nonsense, with the express purpose of confusing Francis still more. A vague meaning can be found.

Notes

Francis was doubtless wearing a white canvas doublet, and the price of sugar (cf. line 60) would be less in Barbary, whence it was originally imported.

II.iv.103,104. *I am not yet of Percy's mind.* The Prince returns to his previous remark, 'I am now of all humors' (94) and qualifies it. The sudden transition from Francis to Hotspur in line 103 is surprising. It is perhaps the feverish activity of the drawer Francis, who is rushing up and down stairs, crying 'anon' in reply to all questions, that reminds the Prince of a similar nervous activity in Hotspur. Shakespeare loses no opportunity of bringing Hal and Hotspur into contrast.

II.iv.121. *Titan.* The sun. Mispunctuation has made this speech obscure in most editions. The phrase 'pitiful-hearted Titan' is parenthetical, as Warburton first suggested, and the clause beginning 'that melted' refers to 'butter.'

II.iv.123. *the sweet tale of the sun's.* The sun's sweet tale. Modern idiom would require 'this sweet tale,' etc.

II.iv.134. *weaver.* Elizabethan weavers were, in large part, 'psalm-singing Puritans,' who had fled to England from the religious persecutions in the Low Countries.

II.iv.176–184. On the confusion of speakers here in the early texts compare note on I.ii.166 and B. H. Bronson, 'A Note on Gadshill, our Setter,' *PMLA*, 1930, pp. 749–753.

II.iv.219. *points.* Falstaff refers to the points of swords. Poins, in his reply, quibblingly interprets points in another sense, namely laces for garments.

II.iv.227. *Kendal green.* A dark green woolen cloth made at Kendal in Westmorland; the traditional costume of Robin Hood.

II.iv.242. *strappado.* A military punishment which consisted of fastening a rope under the arms of the offender, drawing him up by a pulley to the top of a high beam and then suddenly letting him down with a jerk.

II.iv.244. *reasons.* A play on the words *reasons* and *raisins*, which were pronounced alike.

II.iv.272. *By the Lord, I knew ye.* The truth seems to be that whether or not Falstaff recognized the Prince and Poins in their disguise and fled with conviction from the scene of the robbery, in the twelve hours or more during which he was conducting the retreat of his followers from Gadshill to the Boar's Head, he has come to a clear idea of what happened. He therefore enters the inn in the present scene aware of the trick that has

144   The First Part of Henry the Fourth

been played upon him and prepared with a careful plan for turning the situation to the advantage of his own quick wit. Thus he lures Hal and Poins on with Gargantuan lies and evades them with blithe sophistry when they think they have him cornered.

II.iv.295. *royal*. A royal was 10s.; a noble 6s. 8d. Cf. I.ii.144.

II.iv.324–330. Bardolph becomes angry and adopts a threatening attitude. 'My red face,' he implies, 'portends *choler* (anger).' Hal finds it merely a sign of a *hot liver* (caused by drinking) and an empty purse (also caused by drink). When Bardolph insists that it is *choler*, Hal quibblingly interprets *choler* as collar, the hangman's noose or *halter*.

II.iv.341,342. *Amamon . . . Lucifer*. Amaymon was a king of devils, mentioned in Reginald Scot's popular *Discovery of Witchcraft* (1584). *Made Lucifer cuckold* is Falstaff's way of saying that Glendower provided him with his well-known horns (J. Q. Adams).

II.iv.392. *King Cambyses*. A ranting bombastic tragedy by Thomas Preston (1570). Line 396 shows that Falstaff knew more than the name of the play, one line of which reads:
'(*At this tale tolde let the Queene weep.*)

Queene: These wordes to hear makes stilling teares issue from christal eyes.'

II.iv.402. Falstaff may be referring to the Hostess as a pintpot always well filled with tickle-brain, or he may be using tickle-brain not in its technical sense, but merely as an appropriate word for describing the flighty character of the Hostess.

II.iv.403 ff. Falstaff is here burlesquing the somewhat pompous and artificial style of King Henry, and Shakespeare is, at the same time, burlesquing the fashionable and artificial prose style of his own contemporaries, known as Euphuism. This style was exemplified in John Lyly's *Euphues* (1578–1580), and its chief characteristics are: (1) The constant use of antithesis, (2) The use of alliteration to emphasize the antithetic clauses, (3) The frequent use of a long string of similes all relating to the same subject, often taken from the fabulous qualities ascribed to plants, animals, and minerals, (4) The constant use of rhetorical questions, (5) Frequent quotation of proverbs. Falstaff's first figure is taken directly from *Euphues* (ed. Bond, vol. I, p. 196): 'Though the Camomill the more it is trodden and pressed downe, the more it spreadeth, yet the Violet the oftner it is handeled and touched, the sooner it withereth and

Notes

decayeth.' The following passages are good examples of Euphuism: 'Though thou haue eaten the seedes of Rockatte which breede incontinencie, yet haue I chewed the leafe Cresse which mainteineth modestie. Though thou beare in thy bosome the hearbe Araxa most noisome to virginitie, yet haue I the stone that groweth in the mounte Tmolus, the vpholder of chastitie' (Bond, I.222). 'Well doth he know that the glass once crased will with the least clappe be cracked. . . . But can Euphues conuince me of fleetinge, seeing for his sake I breake my fidelitie? Can he condemne me of disloyaltie, when he is the only cause of my dislyking? May he condemn me of trecherye, who hath this testimony as tryall of my good will? Doth he not remember that . . . though the Spyder poyson the Flye, he cannot infect the Bee? That though I have bene light to Philautus, yet I may be louely to Euphues?' (Bond, I. 205–206.)

II.iv.442. Falstaff is comparing himself with the thinnest things he can think of, a young sucking rabbit, or a hare hung up in a poulterer's shop.

II.iv.449. *I'll tickle ye*, etc. This is obviously an aside to Hal, and not part of Falstaff's speech in his rôle of Prince. As he begins his performance, he whispers to Hal, 'My acting of the part of a young prince will tickle you, i' faith.'

II.iv.450,451. *Henceforth ne'er look on me*. Here Hal speaks the words Falstaff dreads. See note on lines 483–485 below.

II.iv.457. *Manningtree ox*. Manningtree is a town in Essex, famous for its fairs at which oxen were roasted whole.

II.iv.478. *Pharaoh's lean kine*. Cf. Genesis 41. 19.

II.iv.483–485. *banish not him thy Harry's company*, etc. This redoubled cry underlines the great fear which lends pathos to Falstaff's effort to make himself an indispensable clown and gives him a kinship with the poet of the Sonnets. Cf. Sonnet 87,

> Farewell! Thou art too dear for my possessing,
> And like enough thou know'st thy estimate.

II.iv.497–499. As in lines 489 ff., Falstaff is loath, even in the face of peril, to forgo his spirited defence of himself (cf. 471–485). He has been hurt by Hal's drastic abuse of him in 450–464, and as the sheriff approaches he makes a last appeal: 'Never miscall one who, like me, is true gold.' 'You, too,' he adds, 'sober though you seem, are essentially a madcap.' (That is, we are brothers under the skin.)

146 The First Part of Henry the Fourth

II.iv.502. *I deny your major.* The syllogism that Falstaff has in mind may run thus:—Major premise: All who run away are natural cowards. Minor premise: Falstaff ran away. Conclusion (stated by Prince): Therefore, Falstaff is a natural coward. Elizabethan schoolboys were well trained in this exercise, and an average audience could probably supply the missing terms. There is also a pun on *major* as here used and maior, the mayor of a town, the officer next in rank above the sheriff.

II.iv.507,508. Falstaff hides behind the curtain which divided the outer from the inner stage in the Elizabethan theatre; the others *walk above*, i.e., on the balcony above the inner stage.

II.iv.519,520. *The man, I do assure you, is not here.* Truth is considerably strained. The man, says the prince, is not here immediately in presence, for I have sent him on a mission behind the arras.

III.i.73. *The archdeacon hath divided it.* Shakespeare found in Holinshed's Chronicle the statement that the deputies of the conspirators divided the realm 'in the house of the Archdeacon of Bangor.' This led Theobald to the quaint idea that the present scene takes place in the Archdeacon of Bangor's house. Shakespeare, who handles the historical situation very freely (the division was not projected till after the deaths of Hotspur and Worcester), evidently assumes the scene to occur in one of Glendower's castles, possibly Penrhyn or Carnarvon, which are both close to Bangor. The value of the archdeacon was that as a clerk he could draw up formal papers and phrase them in Latin.

III.i.100. *the best of all my land.* All Lincolnshire and part of Nottinghamshire. See map. Hotspur's proposal to divert the Trent River is entirely unhistoric. It may have been suggested to Shakespeare by a contemporary disturbance which made a good deal of noise. Sir Thomas Stanhope of Nottinghamshire maintained a weir at Shelford for the purpose of diverting the water of the Trent. On Easter Eve, 1593, 'a great and unlawful assembly of a multitude of persons' gathered together 'in tumultuous and riotous manner' to pull down the weir, and the resulting disorders kept Queen Elizabeth's Privy Council apprehensive for four months. See J. R. Dasent, *Acts of the Privy Council*, New Series, vol. XXIV, pp. 201 ff.

III.i.125. *gave the tongue a helpful ornament.* That is, by learning to sing English poetry to the harp I made my use of the language both effective and graceful.

Notes   147

III.i.149–153. The division of the kingdom was made by the conspirators, according to Holinshed, 'through a foolish credit given to a vain prophecy' that Henry was a moldwarp (a mole) whose kingdom should be divided among a wolf, a dragon, and a lion. This cryptic prophecy was attributed to Merlin, and is referred to in *The Mirror for Magistrates* (1559):

> And for to set us hereon more agog,
> A prophet came (a vengeaunce take them all)
> Affirming Henry to be Gog-magog,
> Whom Merlin doth a mouldwarp ever call,
> Accursed of God, that must be brought in thrall
> By a wulf, a dragon, and a lyon strong,
> Which shuld devide his kingdome them amonge.

Hotspur evidently has not shared in the 'foolish credit' given to the 'vain prophecy' and his only memory of the discussion is that Glendower talked a lot of Celtic nonsense.

III.i.200–203. Mortimer seems to be trying to say that though he does not understand his wife's speech, he understands her looks, and that he is *too perfect* in the language of tears (i.e., *that pretty Welsh* which she pours down from her swollen eyes). So near to tears is the bridegroom himself that shame alone prevents his answering his wife's tears with tears.

III.i.256. *Finsbury.* Archery grounds just outside London, a favorite resort of respectable middle-class citizens.

III.i.258. *velvet-guards.* Velvet trimmings; hence women that wear such finery, notably wives of aldermen.

III.i.261. *tailor.* Tailors, like weavers (cf. II.iv.134n.), were noted for singing at their work.

III.ii.23–28. *As, in reproof,* etc. That, in rebuke of the many falsehoods alleged against me, I may, on showing penitence, find pardon for some real faults of my youth.

III.ii.50. I assumed, or took upon myself, a heavenly graciousness of bearing.

III.ii.62. *carded.* To card was to mix different kinds of drink; so King Richard mixed his high state and dignity with baseness.

III.ii.99. Hal's claim to the crown is shadowy compared with Hotspur's, for Hal's claim is that of inheritance from a usurper who has been rewarded with the crown for his services to the state; whereas Hotspur's claim is that of efficient public service, performed by himself.

III.ii.103. *being no more in debt to years than thou.* Shakespeare's unhistorical assumption for dramatic effect. Hotspur was actually of King Henry's age.

III.ii.164. *Lord Mortimer of Scotland.* Shakespeare's error for George Dunbar, whom Holinshed calls 'the Scot, the Earl of March.' In England, but not in Scotland, the title, Earl of March, ran in the Mortimer family.

III.iii.9. *brewer's horse.* The point of this comparison lies probably in the fact that a brewer's horse carries good liquor on his back, instead of in his belly. They were the lowest of the horse kind.

III.iii.31. It was the fashion to wear, as a *memento mori*, reminder of death, a ring or pin on the stone of which was engraved a skull and cross-bones.

III.iii.33. *Dives that lived in purple.* See St. Luke's Gospel, 16. 19–31.

III.iii.36. Cf. Psalm 104. 4: 'Who maketh his angels spirits; his ministers a flaming fire.'

III.iii.54. *Partlet.* The name of the hen in the famous story of the Cock and the Fox; cf. Chaucer's *Nonnes Preestes Tale.* The hen-like characteristics of the Hostess are apparent in the conversation immediately following.

III.iii.60. *tithe.* Lewis Theobald's emendation for 'tight.'

III.iii.117. *Maid Marian.* The mistress of Robin Hood, often impersonated by a man in the morris-dances, in which she was traditionally a rather disreputable person. 'As regards womanliness,' says Falstaff to the Hostess, 'in comparison with you, Maid Marian is as respectable a person as the wife of the deputy-alderman of this ward.'

III.iii.166. *injuries.* 'As the pocketing of injuries was a common phrase, I suppose the Prince calls the contents of Falstaff's pockets injuries' (Steevens). Cf. 167,168. Hal is sardonically implying that the alleged riches of Falstaff's pockets are all things he is better without.

III.iii.190. *unwashed hands.* Without stopping to wash your hands, i.e., at once; or, possibly, without any over-fastidious scruples.

III.iii.213. *drum.* Used here in the sense of rallying-point or recruiting station.

IV.i.4,5. Another figurative expression referring to coinage; cf. II.iii.91–93. 'Your fame would circulate more widely than that of any soldier of this season's coinage.'

IV.i.56. 'The comfort of having something to fall back upon.'

Notes

IV.i.98. *estridges that woo the wind.* Ostriches increase their speed on ground by receiving the wind into their open wings. The early editions all read 'with' instead of *woo*. The assumption behind the present emendation is that the original printer did not understand the image and misread the verb as the preposition, which was often written 'wth.' Ostrich feathers are (and were) the Prince of Wales's cognizance.

IV.i.99. *Bating.* Again the early editions agree in a senseless form, 'Baited' or 'Bayted.' The printer seems to have been misled by the past participles he had set up in the previous lines and by the following one in *bath'd*. Note that the shift to the present participle is continued in *Glittering* (line 100), and that 'Baited . . . bath'd' would make a very inharmonious verse.

IV.i.100. *images.* The reference is probably to the gilded robes which adorn the images of the saints in churches.

IV.i.101. *As full of spirit as the month of May.* It is hard not to believe that Shakespeare is again consciously remembering Chaucer's Prologue. Compare the latter's description of his Squire (*Prol.* 92),

He was as fresshe as is the month of May.

IV.i.111,112. 'Your praise of him causes me greater fever than the ague in spring.'

IV.i.114. *fire-ey'd maid.* Bellona, goddess of war.

IV.ii.3. *Sutton Cophill.* Sutton Coldfield, a town twenty-four miles northwest of Coventry.

IV.ii.6. 'makes an angel, or ten shillings, that I have spent.'

IV.ii.8. *answer the coinage.* Guarantee that they are not counterfeit (as of course they would not be, being figments of Falstaff's imagination).

IV.ii.12. *I have misused the king's press damnably.* An epidemic of graft in connection with the enlistment of troops for service in France and Ireland gave this scene contemporary topical value. For Captain Joshua Hilliard's peculations from one hundred and fifty men levied in Gloucestershire in 1593 see G. B. Harrison, *An Elizabethan Journal*, vol. i, p. 231 f. Falstaff is here not merely exposing his original sin; he is acting as a humorous commentator on the news.

IV.ii.34. St. Luke's Gospel, 15. 15, 16.

IV.ii.42. *but a shirt.* An emendation of Nicholas Rowe, Shakespeare's first editor (1674–1718). The early texts have 'not a shirt.'

IV.iii.24. *half himself.* Emended by George Steevens (1736–

The First Part of Henry the Fourth

1800). Nearly all texts have 'half of himself,' which destroys the line.

V.i.S.d. The early texts include among the characters in this scene the Earl of Westmorland, who, according to V.ii.28,29, cannot be there.

V.i.13. *old limbs.* The historical King Henry was thirty-seven years old at the time of the battle of Shrewsbury; the historical Hotspur was about forty; and the historical Prince Hal seventeen. The King of Shakespeare's play is, however, an elderly man, and Hotspur and Hal are both young. I.i.87–89 shows that Shakespeare regarded his two youthful heroes as of the same age; and III.ii.112,113 would indicate that they were very young.

V.i.60,61. The cuckoo frequently lays her eggs in the hedge-sparrow's nest; and the hedge-sparrow brings up the young cuckoos, until they have grown 'to such a bulk' that they destroy their foster-parents. Cf. *Lear,* I.iv.221,222:

> The hedge-sparrow fed the cuckoo so long
> That it's had it head bit off by it young.

V.i.126,127. There is probably a pun here on the words death and debt which were pronounced similarly.

V.ii.8. *Suspicion.* Another emendation of Rowe (1714) for 'Supposition' in all the early copies. As emended the line is an impressive alexandrine, well suited to emphasize the gravity of Worcester's warning. The immediate source of the image in this line is Spenser's *Faerie Queene* (I.iv.31), where Envy is 'ypainted full of eyes.'

V.ii.71. *a libertine.* Emendation of Edward Capell (1713–1781). The first Quarto has 'a libertie'; the fifth Quarto and Folio 'at libertie.'

V.ii.100.S.d. At this point modern editors, mistakenly, begin a new scene. The stage direction shows Shakespeare's intention. The spectacle of Hotspur's army embracing merges with the other spectacle of the entrance of the king's army. For a time the stage is crowded with fighting figures, who gradually disappear as in a dance movement. Then, immediately, Douglas and Blunt return to face each other on the empty stage.

V.ii.101. *What is thy name, that in battle thus?* The line lacks a syllable, but is probably as Shakespeare wrote it. He sometimes uses trochaic rhythms to give the sense of brusque or violent movement, as in the opening lines of the witches in *Macbeth*.

Notes

V.ii.120. *his name was Blunt.* It is perhaps surprising that Hotspur does not remember introducing Sir Walter Blunt to Douglas on the day before. See IV.iii.32.

V.ii.122. *'fool' go with thy soul.* May that epithet accompany you to the next world.

V.ii.145. *Turk Gregory.* Editors all agree that Falstaff here refers to Pope Gregory VII, Hildebrand, who, as a friar, was famous for violent exploits. Attempts to explain the appellation Turk are not very satisfactory. Falstaff perhaps has in mind the phrase 'to fight like a Turk.'

V.ii.156. Another pun. The -ie- of pierce was pronounced like the -e- of Percy.

V.iii.65. A reference to Ptolemaic astronomy, according to which each planet was fixed in a crystal sphere with which it revolved.

V.iii.96. *favors.* Here probably used for the Prince's ostrich feathers, the badge of his rank, which he removes from his helmet. See H. Hartman, 'Prince Hal's "Shew of Zeale",' *PMLA*, 1931, pp. 720–723.

V.iii.114. *termagant.* Name of one of the fabled idols worshipped by Mohammedans, according to mediæval romance.

V.iii.160. *Come, brother, let us to the highest of the field.* The word *brother* is 'extra-metrical'; that is, the verse line is complete without it. The addition of such words, normally words of direct address, was one of the allowable variations in dramatic blank verse.

V.iii.162. *I'll follow, as they say, for reward.* Falstaff returns, with better expectations, to the vocation in which we first see him (I.ii), that of suitor for court patronage.

APPENDIX A

SOURCES OF THE PLAY

The sources of the serious plot of both parts of Shakespeare's *Henry IV* are (1) the 1587 edition of *The Chronicles of England, Scotland, and Ireland* by Raphael Holinshed 'of Bromecote in the County of Warr(wick)'; and (2) either Samuel Daniel's poem, *The Civile Wars between the two Houses of Lancaster and York* (1595) or some lost poem, play, or chronicle followed by both Daniel and Shakespeare.

The source of the comic plot is a crude and slight chronicle play called *The Famous Victories of Henry V*, acted as early as 1588 and entered for publication in 1594.

Selections from Holinshed's Account of the Battle of Shrewsbury[1]

The next day in the morning early, being the even of Mary Magdalene [21 July, 1403], they set their battles in order on both sides, and now, whilest the warriors looked when the token of battle should be given, the abbot of Shrewsbury, and one of the clerks of the privy seal, were sent from the king unto the Percies, to offer them pardon, if they would come to any reasonable agreement. By their persuasions, the lord Henry Percy began to give ear unto the king's offers, & so sent with them his

[1] Spelling modernized.

Appendix A

uncle the Earl of Worcester, to declare unto the king the causes of those troubles. . . .

It was reported for a truth, that now when the king had condescended unto all that was reasonable at his hands to be required, and seemed to humble himself more than was meet for his estate, the Earl of Worcester (upon his return to his nephew) made relation clean contrary to that the king had said, in such sort that he set his nephew's heart more in displeasure towards the king than ever it was before; driving him by that means to fight whether he would or not. . . .

And forthwith the Lord Percy, as a captain of high courage, began to exhort the captains and soldiers to prepare themselves to battle, sith the matter was grown to that point, that by no means it could be avoided, 'so that,' said he, 'this day shall either bring us all to advancement & honor, or else if it shall chance us to be overcome, shall deliver us from the king's spiteful malice and cruel disdain: for playing the men (as we ought to do), better it is to die in battle for the commonwealth's cause, than through cowardlike fear to prolong life, which after shall be taken from us by the sentence of the enemy. . . .'

Then suddenly blew the trumpets, the king's part crying, 'St. George! Upon them!' the adversaries cried *'Esperance! Percy!'* and so the two armies furiously joined. . . .

The prince that day helped his father like a lusty young gentleman; for although he was hurt in the face with an arrow, so that diverse noblemen that were about him would have conveyed him forth of the field, yet he would not suffer them so to do, lest his departure from amongst his men might happily have stricken some fear into their hearts: and so without regard of his hurt, he continued

154 The First Part of Henry the Fourth

with his men, & never ceased either to fight where the battle was most hot, or to encourage his men where it seemed most need.

Selections from Daniel's Civil Wars (1595), Book III (The Battle of Shrewsbury)

Stanza 100
And yet undaunted Hotspur, seeing the king
So near approach'd, leaving the work in hand . . .
Brings a strong host of firm resolved might,
And plac'd his troops before the king in sight.

St. 101
'This day' (saith he), 'O faithful valiant friends,
Whatever it doth give, shall glory give:
This day with honor frees our state, or ends
Our misery with fame that still shall live.
And do but think how well this day he spends
That spends his blood his country to relieve:
Our holy cause, our freedom, and our right
Sufficient are to move good minds to fight.'

St. 107
But now begin these fury-moving sounds
The notes of wrath that music brought from hell,
The rattling drums which trumpet's voice confounds,
The cries, th'encouragements, the shouting shrell,
That all about the beaten air rebounds,
Thund'ring confused murmurs horrible . . .

Appendix A

St. 110

There, lo that new-appearing glorious star,
Wonder of arms, the terror of the field,
Young Henry, laboring where the stoutest are,
And even the stoutest forces back to yield . . .

St. 113

And dear it cost, and O much blood is shed
To purchase thee this losing victory,
O travailed King. Yet hast thou conquered
A doubtful day, a mighty enemy.
But O what wounds! what famous worth lies dead!
That makes the winner look with sorrowing eye:
Magnanimous Stafford lost, that much had wrought,
And valiant Shorly, who great glory got.

St. 114

Such wrack of others' blood thou didst behold,
O furious Hotspur, ere thou lost thine own!
Which now once lost, that heat in thine waxt cold,
And soon became thy army overthrown.
And O that this great spirit, this courage bold,
Had in some good cause been rightly shown!
So had not we thus violently then
Have term'd that rage which valor should have been.

SELECTION FROM THE FAMOUS VICTORIES OF
HENRY V [1]

The following is the first conversation [2] between Prince Hal and Falstaff (Sir John Oldcastle):

[1] For complete text see J. Q. Adams, *Chief Pre-Shakespearean Dramas*, pp. 667–690.
[2] Spelling modernized. Compare Shakespeare's play, I. ii. 59 ff.

Enter Sir John Old-Castle.

Hen. 5. How now Sir John Old-Castle,
What news with you?

Joh. Old. I am glad to see your Grace at liberty,[3]
I was come, I, to visit you in prison.

Hen. 5. To visit me? Didst thou not know that I am a Prince's son? . . . But I tell you, sirs, when I am king we will have no such things. But, my lads, if the old king, my father, were dead, we would all be kings.

Joh. Old. He is a good old man; God take him to his mercy the sooner.

Hen. 5. But, Ned, so soon as I am king, the first thing I will do, shall be to put my Lord Chief Justice out of office. And thou shalt be my Lord Chief Justice of England.

Ned. Shall I be Lord Chief Justice? By gogs wounds, I'll be the bravest Lord Chief Justice that ever was in England.

Hen. 5. Thou shalt hang none but pickpurses and horse-stealers and such base-minded villains. But that fellow that will stand by the highway side courageously with his sword and buckler and take a purse, that fellow—give him commendations! Beside that, send him to me and I will give him an annual pension out of my Exchequer.

---

[3] The Prince had just been committed to the Fleet Prison for striking the Lord Chief Justice.

APPENDIX B

THE HISTORY OF THE PLAY

1 Henry IV was apparently written in the year 1597, when Shakespeare completed his thirty-third year. He had probably already produced ten or twelve successful plays, among them *Romeo and Juliet* and *The Merchant of Venice*. The year 1596 had witnessed the English expedition to Spain and the capture of the city of Cadiz; the year 1597 saw the 'Islands Voyage,' another grandiose adventure under the command of the mercurial and Hotspur-like Earl of Essex. English patriotism never found nobler expression than in the historical plays of Shakespeare written during these years of national trial and endeavor.

In Shakespeare's first version of the play he evidently retained the name Oldcastle for the fat knight who attended the Prince. Hal's pun, 'my old lad of the castle' (I. ii. 42, 43) probably bears witness to this, as does the metrical imperfection in the line

Away, good Ned. Falstaff sweats to death (II. ii. 107)

which would be corrected by the substitution of the word Oldcastle for Falstaff. In the first Quarto of *2 Henry IV*, the prefix *Old.* is found instead of *Fal.* before Falstaff's speech in I. ii. 137, and in the Epilogue to this play the author explicitly states that the Falstaff of the play is not the Oldcastle who 'died a martyr.' Despite this disclaimer, audiences seem long to have referred to *1 Henry IV* as 'the play of Oldcastle.'

Oldcastle was a famous Lollard, and according to tradition many Elizabethan Protestants (including Lord Cobham, the Lord Chamberlain) protested against Shakespeare's degradation of an honorable name, and 'some of that family being then remaining, the Queen was pleased to command him to alter it.' It is at least a singular coincidence that Shakespeare substituted the name of a Lollard sympathizer, Sir John Fastolfe, in slightly disguised form. The Falstaff of the play bears little resemblance, save in name, to either Sir John Oldcastle or Sir John Fastolfe.

Of the first performances and the first players of *Henry IV* no records are extant; but the large number of contemporary references give testimony to the fact of the play's popularity. Ben Jonson alludes to the fatness of Sir John Falstaff in the curtain-line of his *Every Man out of his Humour* (1599), and in Beaumont and Fletcher's *Knight of the Burning Pestle* (c. 1610), Ralph, the apprentice, when asked to 'speak a huffing part,' declaims Hotspur's speech on honor, with variations. Shakespeare's chief rivals, the Lord Admiral's players, in 1599 paid him the compliment of producing two plays of their own on *The Life of Sir John Oldcastle*; and even during the period of the Commonwealth, Puritan legislation failed to prevent the clandestine performance of a farcical abridgment of Shakespeare's play, known as *The Bouncing Knight*. Professor Bentley has calculated that through the whole seventeenth century Falstaff was the most popular of all stage characters.[1]

---

[1] G. E. Bentley, *Shakespeare and Jonson: Their Reputations in the Seventeenth Century Compared* (1945).

Appendix B

John Lowin (1576–1659) is the earliest actor whose name is associated with the play. James Wright in his *Historia Histrionica* (1699) says that 'before the wars' Lowin acted Falstaff 'with mighty applause.' Lowin seems to have joined Shakespeare's company in 1603, six or seven years after the probable date of the first performance of *Henry IV*.

This play was one of the first to be revived publicly after the Restoration. Pepys first saw it in December, 1660, and was disappointed,—'my expectation being too great, . . . and my having a book I believe did spoil it a little.' The next spring, however, Pepys saw it again, and pronounced it 'a good play.' In November, 1667, and September, 1668, Pepys attended performances again, and 'contrary to expectation was pleased in nothing more than in Cartwright's speaking of Falstaff's speech about "What is Honor?"'

During the seventies John Lacey succeeded Cartwright in the rôle of Falstaff; and in 1682, the year after Lacey's death, at the time of the union of the King's and the Duke's players, the great Thomas Betterton appeared as Hotspur. Eighteen years later, at the age of sixty-five, Betterton appeared as Falstaff 'which drew all the town more than any new play produced of late. . . . The critics allow that Betterton has hit the humor of Falstaff better than any that have aimed at it before, . . . though he lacks the waggery of Estcourt, the drollery of Harper, and the salaciousness of Jack Evans.' (Genest, II, 381; V. 596.) Six notable Falstaffs in one generation is a record of which the seventeenth century may be proud.

Betterton's acting version of the play was published in 1700. Genest notes that he 'judiciously retains' the conversation of Falstaff and the Prince in Act Second, and also the first scene in Act Third, although he omits the character of Lady Mortimer. The obvious inference to be drawn from Genest's opening remark is indeed astounding, namely, that it had been the custom, before Betterton's time, to cut the great Boar's Head Tavern scene. But it was after Betterton's time that, according to Genest, a 'happy (sic) addition' was made to Falstaff's speech which begins 'By the Lord, I knew ye as well as he that made ye' by prefixing the question 'Do ye think that I did not know ye?' This singularly infelicitous addition to Shakespeare's text was retained by Sir Herbert Tree in his performance of the Boar's Head Tavern scene at the Shakespeare Tercentenary Festival in the New Amsterdam Theatre, New York, in April, 1916.

Verbruggen was Betterton's Hotspur, and according to Genest (II. 381) he was 'nature without extravagance, and freedom without licentiousness,—he was vociferous without bellowing.' The inference to be drawn with respect to former performances is again interesting.

Twenty other actors are known to have played Falstaff between 1700 and 1750, and the play-bills of twenty performances of *1 Henry IV* between 1706 and 1826 are in existence. Six of these performances were at the Haymarket, seven at Drury Lane, two at Lincoln's Inn Fields, and five at Covent Garden.

Garrick first appeared as Hotspur at the Covent Garden performance in 1746, his rival, Quin, appearing as Falstaff, a rôle in which he had made himself a name eight years before. We are told that 'the advantage was greatly on Quin's side, as the part of Hotspur was not suited to Garrick's figure or style of acting.'

Henderson was the great Falstaff of the latter half of the eighteenth century, and played at the Haymarket, Drury Lane, and Covent Garden. He is said to have made Falstaff 'neither very vulgar nor very polite.' An entirely unique performance must have been that of 1786 when Mrs. Webb appeared as Falstaff in a 'benefit' for herself.

In 1818 William Charles Macready (1793–1873) succeeded the aging and long famous John Philip Kemble as Hotspur at the Drury Lane Theatre; while Kemble's younger brother, Charles, appeared as Falstaff in the 1824 production at Covent Garden. 'He endeavored to rescue the part from coarseness. In the presence of the king and in the conversation with Westmorland, he invested it with gentility and courtly bearing.'

Another popular Falstaff of the early nineteenth century was George Bartley, who made his first appearance in the rôle in 1815. 'His success was equal to his most sanguine expectations, and richly merited.' Bartley made a triumphal tour of America in 1818–1819, and gave instruction in reading and elocution in many American colleges. In 'Hertford,' the capital of Connecticut, he and his accomplished wife were arrested for indulging in dramatic readings, one Ebenezer Huntington, a puritanical Attorney General, having resurrected one of Connecticut's famous blue laws for this purpose.

After Bartley's farewell performance in 1852, there were few revivals of Henry IV, and the play, which for two centuries had been almost continuously acted, nearly disappeared from the stage, except for the sterling productions of Samuel Phelps (1804–1878) and later of the Old Vic company, and in America of Otis Skinner (1858–1942). One may perhaps hold the 'Shakespeare idolaters' of the school of Lamb and Hazlitt partly to blame. In their transcendental enthusiasm they insisted upon a Falstaff as huge in mind as in body, and they ended by pushing him over the whole play and beyond the grasp of the mere actor. The inclusion of *1 Henry IV* in the repertoires of Sir Herbert Tree and of Sir Francis Benson's company at the Stratford Memorial Theatre did little for its fame; and Julia Marlowe's production in 1896 drew from New York critics the opinion that the play is inherently 'unactable.' But there are clear signs that it is returning to the boards. The Margaret Webster arrangement in 1939, with Maurice Evans as Falstaff and with some intrusions from *Part Two*, ran for seventy-four performances in New York, and the full-length production of both parts in 1945 by Laurence Olivier and the Old Vic company (on visit from London) was one of the most unquestioned successes that Shakespeare has had on the New York stage.

Index of Words Glossed

(Figures in full-faced type refer to page-numbers)

accidents: 25 (1.2.213)
admiral: 90 (3.3.26)
adopted: 119 (5.2.18)
advantage: 72 (2.4.555)
advertisement (advice): **99** (4.1.36)
advertisement (information): **89** (3.2.172)
affections: 84 (3.2.30)
against his name: 85 (3.2.65)
albeit: 31 (1.3.128)
Allhallown summer: 23 (1.2.162, 163); **139**
Amamon: 64 (2.4.341); **144**
amaze: 125 (5.3.6)
ancient: 104 (4.2.31)
ancients: 104 (4.2.23)
angel (God's angel): 91 (3.3.36); **148**
angel (money): 103 (4.2.6); **149**
and if: 30 (1.3.125)
answer the coinage: 103 (4.2.8); **149**
Antic: 20 (1.2.62)
apple-john: 89 (3.3.4)
appointment: 24 (1.2.179)
apprehends: 34 (1.3.209)
approve: 98 (4.1.9)
approved: 15 (1.1.54)
arbitrement: 100 (4.1.70)
argument: 46 (2.2.94)
arras: 70 (2.4.507)
art: 74 (3.1.48)
articulate: 116 (5.1.72)
as: 104 (4.2.32)
as in a castle: 41 (2.1.86)
as well: 83 (3.2.20)
aspects: 16 (1.1.97); **137**
attended: 109 (4.3.70)
athwart: 14 (1.1.36)
attribution: 97 (4.1.3)

bacons: 45 (2.2.90)
baffle: 21 (1.2.104)
balk'd: 15 (1.1.69)
bands: 88 (3.2.157)
banes: 103 (4.2.17)
basilisks: 49 (2.3.54)
bastard: 52 (2.4.27)
bastinado: 64 (2.4.341)
bate: 89 (3.3.2)
bating: 101 (4.1.99); **149**
bavin: 85 (3.2.61)
be your speed: 79 (3.1.190)
beaver: 101 (4.1.104)
beguiling: 79 (3.1.189)
beholding: 41 (2.1.88)
beldam: 73 (3.1.32)
bestride: 117 (5.1.122)
bide the touch: 111 (4.4.10)
big: 100 (4.1.58)
blood: 79 (3.1.181)
blown: 105 (4.2.49)
book: 80 (3.1.224)
bootless: 14 (1.1.29); **74** (3.1.68)
boots: 41 (2.1.82)
bots: 38 (2.1.9)
bottom: 76 (3.1.106)
brach: 81 (3.1.239)
brave: 20 (1.2.66)
brawn: 56 (2.4.112)
break with: 77 (3.1.144)
breathe in watering: 52 (2.4.16)
brewer's horse: 90 (3.3.9); **148**
brief: 111 (4.4.1)
Bring in: 19 (1.2.37)
Bristow: 36 (1.3.269)
Bolingbroke: 31 (1.3.137); **139**
bolters: 92 (3.3.72)
bolting-hutch: 68 (2.4.455)
bombard: 68 (2.4.456)
bombast: 63 (2.4.332)
bluecaps: 64 (2.4.362)

164   Index of Words Glossed

broached: 114 (5.1.21)
buckler: 35 (1.3.230)
buckram: 24 (1.2.183)
buff jerkin: 19 (1.2.43); 138
busky: 113 (5.1.2)
but: 127 (5.3.43)

caddis: 54 (2.4.71)
caliver: 104 (4.2.19)
Cambyses': 65 (2.4.392); 144
camomile: 66 (2.4.405)
candy: 35 (1.3.250)
canker: 32 (1.3.176)
canker'd: 31 (1.3.137)
cankers: 104 (4.2.30)
cannot choose: 77 (3.1.148)
canstick: 77 (3.1.131)
cantle: 76 (3.1.101)
capital: 87 (3.2.110)
capitulate: 87 (3.2.120)
carbonado: 125 (5.2.158)
carded: 85 (3.2.62); 147
cart: 70 (2.4.503)
case: 44 (2.2.52)
cases: 24 (1.2.183)
cates: 78 (3.1.163)
cess: 38 (2.1.7)
chamberlain: 40 (2.1.47)
chamber-lie: 39 (2.1.20)
changing: 30 (1.3.101)
channel: 13 (1.1.7)
charge (baggage): 40 (2.1.46)
charge (expense): 76 (3.1.113)
charge (provisions): 14 (1.1.35)
charge of foot: 71 (2.4.552)
Charing Cross: 39 (2.1.25); 141
Charles' wain: 38 (2.1.2); 141
cheap: 91 (3.3.47)
chewet: 114 (5.1.29)
chides: 74 (3.1.45)
choler: 31 (1.3.129)
choose: 77 (3.1.148)
chops: 22 (1.2.139)
chuffs: 45 (2.2.89)
cital: 121 (5.2.61)
clerks: 40 (2.1.62); 141
clipt in: 74 (3.1.44)
cloak-bag: 68 (2.4.457)
close: 13 (1.1.13)
close (grapple): 13 (1.1.13)
close (out of sight): 42 (2.2.3)
cloudy: 86 (3.2.83)
coinage: 103 (4.2.8); 149
color (disguise): 30 (1.3.109)
color (pretext): 86 (3.2.100)
colt: 43 (2.2.37)

comfit-maker: 82 (3.1.252)
commodity: 20 (1.2.86)
community: 85 (3.2.77)
comparative: 20 (1.2.83); 85 (3.2.67)
concealments: 78 (3.1.167)
condition: 26 (1.3.6)
conduct: 75 (3.1.93)
confound: 30 (1.3.100)
conjunction: 99 (4.1.37)
contagious: 25 (1.2.204)
continent: 76 (3.1.111)
Corinthian: 52 (2.4.12)
corpes: 15 (1.1.43)
corrival: 34 (1.3.207)
countenance: 18 (1.2.29); 137
cousin: 37 (1.3.290)
coz: 16 (1.1.91)
cozeners: 36 (1.3.254)
cozening: 22 (1.2.125)
crack'd crowns: 50 (2.3.94); 142
cranking: 76 (3.1.99)
cressets: 73 (3.1.15)
crisp: 30 (1.3.106)
crowns: 50 (2.3.94)
cry you mercy: 34 (1.3.212)
current (in circulation): 98 (4.1.5); 148
current (true): 40 (2.1.54)
currents: 49 (2.3.56)
curst: 48 (2.3.47)
cushes: 101 (4.1.105)
Cut: 38 (2.1.5)

daff'd: 101 (4.1.96)
damnable iteration: 21 (1.2.93); 138
dangerous: 115 (5.1.69)
dank: 38 (2.1.8)
dare we: 117 (5.1.101)
deal: 35 (1.3.250)
dear (affectionate): 129 (5.3.95)
dear (valued): 112 (4.4.31)
dear expedience: 14 (1.1.33)
dearest (best): 133 (5.4.36)
dearest (most valuable): 79 (3.1.182)
defend: 108 (4.3.38)
defy (despise): 98 (4.1.6)
defy (renounce): 35 (1.3.228)
deliver: 119 (5.2.26)
deliver up: 119 (5.2.28)
deliver'd: 27 (1.3.26)
denier: 92 (3.3.81)
dial's point: 121 (5.2.83)

Index of Words Glossed

Diana's: 18 (1.2.25)
discontents: 116 (5.1.76)
disdain'd: 33 (1.3.183)
disputation: 80 (3.1.205)
distemperature: 113 (5.1.3)
Dives: 91 (3.3.33); 148
divide myself: 48 (2.3.33); 142
division: 80 (3.1.210)
dole: 45 (2.2.76)
doom: 83 (3.2.6)
doubtless: 83 (3.2.20)
dowlas: 92 (3.3.71)
draff: 104 (4.2.35)
draws: 100 (4.1.73)
drawers: 52 (2.4.7)
drawn fox: 94 (3.3.116)
drench: 55 (2.4.109)
drum: 97 (3.3.213); 148
durance: 19 (1.2.44); 138
duties of a man: 120 (5.2.55)

Earl of March: 29 (1.3.84)
Eastcheap: 22 (1.2.133); 138
ecce signum: 58 (2.4.171)
ell: 92 (3.3.74)
embossed: 95 (3.3.162)
embowell'd: 129 (5.3.109)
enfeoff'd: 85 (3.2.69)
engag'd: 110 (4.3.95)
egg and butter: 18 (1.2.21)
engross up: 88 (3.2.148)
enlarged: 87 (3.2.115)
enlargement: 73 (3.1.31)
equity stirring: 46 (2.2.99)
Esperance: 49 (2.3.72)
estimation (conjecture): 36 (1.3.270)
estimation (reputation): 112 (4.4.32)
estridges: 101 (4.1.98); 149
even: 37 (1.3.283)
exhalations: 63 (2.4.325)
exhal'd: 114 (5.1.19)
expedience: 14 (1.1.33)
extenuation: 83 (3.2.22)

face: 116 (5.1.74)
factor: 88 (3.2.147)
fadom-line: 33 (1.3.204)
fall off: 29 (1.3.94)
father: 66 (2.4.397)
fat room: 51 (2.4.1); 142
favors (badge): 129 (5.3.96); 151
favors (features): 87 (3.2.136)
faz'd: 104 (4.2.31)

fearful: 100 (4.1.67)
fernseed: 41 (2.1.87); 142
figures: 34 (1.3.209)
fine: 97 (4.1.2)
Finsbury: 82 (3.1.256); 147
fire-ey'd maid: 102 (4.1.114); 149
flight: 84 (3.2.31)
flocks: 38 (2.1.6)
foot of fear: 132 (5.4.20)
foot land-rakers: 41 (2.1.73); 141
forswearing: 120 (5.2.38)
forsworn: 120 (5.2.38)
forward: 44 (2.2.47)
found me: 26 (1.3.3)
franklin: 40 (2.1.54)
from the flight: 84 (3.2.31)
frontier: 26 (1.3.19)
frontiers: 49 (2.3.53)
fubbed: 19 (1.2.61)
furnish'd: 101 (4.1.97)
furniture: 97 (3.3.208)

Gadshill: 21 (1.2.109); 138
gage: 32 (1.3.173)
garters: 44 (2.2.43); 142
gelding: 76 (3.1.111)
gib cat: 20 (1.2.77)
give us leave: 82 (3.2.1)
God save the mark: 28 (1.3.56); 139
God's angel: 91 (3.3.36); 148
good night: 33 (1.3.194)
gorbellied: 45 (2.2.88)
government: 79 (3.1.184)
grace: 18 (1.2.17); 137
grief: 28 (1.3.51)
gull: 115 (5.1.60); 150
gummed velvet: 42 (2.2.2); 142
gurnet: 103 (4.2.12)
gyves: 104 (4.2.41)

habits: 24 (1.2.179)
hair: 100 (4.1.61)
half-fac'd: 34 (1.3.208)
half himself: 107 (4.3.24); 149
Half-moon: 52 (2.4.28)
half-sword: 57 (2.4.167)
happily: 37 (1.3.295)
happy man be his dole: 45 (2.2.76)
hardiment: 30 (1.3.101)
hare: 20 (1.2.80); 138
harlotry (rascally): 66 (2.4.400)
harlotry (silly girl): 79 (3.1.199)
harness: 86 (3.2.101)
Harry Percy: 15 (1.1.53); 136

Index of Words Glossed

havoc: 116 (5.1.82)
hazard: 31 (1.3.128)
he: 81 (3.1.234)
head: 37 (1.3.282)
head of safety: 110 (4.3.103)
heady: 49 (2.3.56)
hearken'd for: 127 (5.3.52)
heir-apparent garters: 44 (2.2.43); 142
hest: 49 (2.3.63)
highest: 131 (5.3.160); 151
highly penn'd: 80 (3.1.208)
hilts: 59 (2.4.211)
hind: 47 (2.3.16)
hitherto: 75 (3.1.75)
hold a wing: 84 (3.2.30)
holds current: 40 (2.1.53,54)
holiday . . . terms: 28 (1.3.46)
holland: 92 (3.3.73)
Holy-rood day: 15 (1.1.52); 136
homo: 42 (2.1.95); 142
hot in question: 14 (1.1.34)
hot livers: 63 (2.4.328); 144
humor (caprice): 25 (1.2.202)
humor (inclination): 20 (1.2.72)
humorous: 81 (3.1.234)
humors: 68 (2.4.455)
Hybla: 19 (1.2.42)
Hydra: 126 (5.3.25)

ignis fatuus: 91 (3.3.40)
images: 101 (4.1.100); 149
impeach: 29 (1.3.75)
impressed: 14 (1.1.21)
in the neck: 109 (4.3.92)
in us: 31 (1.3.149)
incomprehensible: 24 (1.2.191)
indent: 29 (1.3.87)
indenture: 53 (2.4.48)
indentures: 75 (3.1.81)
indirect: 110 (4.3.105)
induction: 72 (3.1.2)
injuries: 95 (3.3.166); 148
innovation: 116 (5.1.78)
intelligence: 110 (4.3.98)
interchangeably: 75 (3.1.82)
interest: 86 (3.2.98)
intestine: 13 (1.1.12)
irregular: 14 (1.1.40)
it: 117 (5.1.115)
iteration: 21 (1.2.93); 138

John of Gaunt: 44 (2.2.66); 142
jordan: 39 (2.1.19)
journey-bated: 107 (4.3.26)

jumps: 20 (1.2.71)
jure: 45 (2.2.91)
justling: 98 (4.1.18)

Kendal green: 60 (2.4.227); **143**
kept: 35 (1.3.244)
kind: 30 (1.3.121)
king christen: 39 (2.1.17)
king's press: 103 (4.2.12); 149
knotty-pated: 60 (2.4.232)

lad of the castle: 19 (1.2.42); 157
lady terms: 28 (1.3.46)
Lancaster: 72 (3.1.8)
latter spring: 23 (1.2.162); **139**
Lay by: 19 (1.2.37)
Lazarus: 104 (4.2.25)
leading: 107 (4.3.17)
leaping-houses: 17 (1.2.9)
leash: 52 (2.4.7)
leave: 133 (5.4.44)
leg: 65 (2.4.393)
lett'st slip: 36 (1.3.276)
libertine: 15 (5.2.71); 150
liking: 90 (3.3.6)
limits: 14 (1.1.35)
line (rank): 32 (1.3.168)
line (strengthen): 50 (2.3.84)
links: 91 (3.3.44)
liquored: 41 (2.1.85); 142
list: 99 (4.1.51)
livery: 108 (4.3.62)
loach: 39 (2.1.21)
long-staff sixpenny strikers: 41 (2.1.74); 141
look when: 35 (1.3.252); 141
loop: 100 (4.1.71)
Lord Mortimer of Scotland: 88 (3.2.164); 148
lost: 26 (1.3.8)
lugged bear: 20 (1.2.77)
lustier maintenance: 126 (5.3.22)

Maid Marian: 94 (3.3.117); 148
main: 99 (4.1.47)
mainly: 59 (2.4.204)
major: 69 (2.4.502); 146
majority: 86 (3.2.109)
makes an angel: 103 (4.2.6); 149
make up: 125 (5.3.5)
mak'st some tender: 127 (5.3.49)
malevolent: 16 (1.1.97); 137
mammets: 50 (2.3.93)
manage: 49 (2.3.50)
manent: 117 (5.1.120)

Index of Words Glossed

Manningtree: 68 (2.4.457); 145
mark: 40 (2.1.56)
Marry: 18 (1.2.23)
match: 55 (2.4.92)
match'd: 15 (1.1.49)
medicines: 43 (2.2.19)
meeting: 89 (3.2.174)
memento mori: 90 (3.3.31); 148
Michaelmas: 53 (2.4.55); 142
micher: 66 (2.4.413)
milliner: 27 (1.3.36); 139
mincing: 77 (3.1.134)
minion: 16 (1.1.83)
minions: 18 (1.2.26)
misprision: 27 (1.3.27)
mo: 112 (4.4.31)
moiety: 76 (3.1.97)
moldwarp: 77 (3.1.149); 147
moody: 26 (1.3.19)
Moorditch: 20 (1.2.81); 138
Mordake: 16 (1.1.71); 136
more and less: 109 (4.3.68)
Mortimer: 14 (1.1.38); 136
mouthed wounds: 29 (1.3.97)
murtherous subornation: 32 (1.3.163)
mustachio-purple-hued malt worms: 41 (2.1.75); 141
mutual well-beseeming ranks: 13 (1.1.14)

name: 85 (3.2.65)
neat's-tongue: 60 (2.4.250)
neck: 109 (4.3.92)
nether: 66 (2.4.410)
nether-stocks: 56 (2.4.117)
Newgate: 93 (3.3.92)
next: 38 (2.1.9)
nice: 99 (4.1.48)
nonce: 24 (1.2.184)
noted: 24 (1.2.184)
not-pated: 54 (2.4.71)

ob.: 71 (2.4.546)
obedient orb: 114 (5.1.17)
offering side: 100 (4.1.69)
oneyers: 41 (2.1.76); 141
opinion (arrogance): 79 (3.1.135)
opinion (prestige): 100 (4.1.77)
opinion (public opinion): 84 (3.2.42)
opposed continent: 76 (3.1.111)
or . . . or: 119 (5.2.12)
or sink or swim: 33 (1.3.194)
orb: 114 (5.1.17)

ornament: 77 (3.1.125); 146
other: 58 (2.4.186)
ought: 94 (3.3.139)
outfaced: 61 (2.4.261)
owe: 121 (5.2.67)

paid: 58 (2.4.195)
painted cloth: 104 (4.2.25)
palisadoes: 49 (2.3.53)
parcel: 55 (2.4.103)
parmaceti: 28 (1.3.58)
participation: 86 (3.2.87)
Partlet: 91 (3.3.54); 148
passages of life: 83 (3.2.8)
passion (deep feeling): 65 (2.4.391)
passion (pain): 73 (3.1.35)
Paul's: 71 (2.4.533)
peach: 44 (2.2.44)
pell-mell havoc: 116 (5.1.82)
peppercorn: 90 (3.3.9)
personal: 109 (4.3.88)
Pharaoh's lean kine: 69 (2.4.478); 145
pierce: 124 (5.2.156); 151
pismires: 35 (1.3.240)
play: 52 (2.4.17)
point: 38 (2.1.6)
points: 59 (2.4.219); 143
Pomgarnet: 53 (2.4.38)
popinjay: 28 (1.3.50)
popularity: 85 (3.2.69)
portly: 26 (1.3.13)
possess'd: 99 (4.1.40)
possession: 84 (3.2.43)
pouncet-box: 27 (1.3.38)
powder: 129 (5.3.112)
precedent: 53 (2.4.33)
predicament: 32 (1.3.168)
present: 79 (3.1.183)
present want: 99 (4.1.44)
presently: 82 (3.2.3)
press: 103 (4.2.12); 149
prodigals: 104 (4.2.34); **149**
profited: 78 (3.1.166)
proof: 44 (2.2.68)
puke: 54 (2.4.71)
pupil age: 55 (2.4.96)
purchase: 42 (2.1.92)
purposes: 113 (5.1.4)
push: 85 (3.2.66)

quality: 108 (4.3.36)
question: 14 (1.1.34)
question'd: 28 (1.3.47)
quiddities: 19 (1.2.46)

Index of Words Glossed

quips: 19 (1.2.46)
quit: 83 (3.2.19)
quite besides: 79 (3.1.179)

range: 32 (1.3.169)
rated: 110 (4.3.99)
rated sinew: 111 (4.4.17)
razes: 39 (2.1.24)
read to: 74 (3.1.46)
reasons: 60 (2.4.244); 143
receipt of fernseed: 41 (2.1.86,87)
reckoning: 55 (2.4.103)
redbreast-teacher: 82 (3.1.261)
reprisal: 102 (4.1.118)
reproof: 24 (1.2.195)
resolution: 19 (1.2.61)
respect: 107 (4.3.31)
retires: 49 (2.3.52)
re-told: 29 (1.3.73)
reversion: 99 (4.1.54)
rightly taken: 63 (2.4.329); 63 (2.4.330)
Rivo: 56 (2.4.112)
roundly: 18 (1.2.22)
royal: 62 (2.4.295); 144

sack: 17 (1.2.3)
St. Nicholas: 40 (2.1.61); 141
salamander: 91 (3.3.48)
sanguine: 60 (2.4.247)
sarcenet: 82 (3.1.254)
saving your reverence: 68 (2.4.474)
'Sblood: 20 (1.2.76)
scope: 78 (3.1.171)
scot and lot: 130 (5.3.114)
Scroop: 36 (1.3.269); 141
scutcheon: 118 (5.1.140)
seek: 126 (5.3.32)
sembably furnish'd: 123 (5.2.121)
serve: 53 (2.4.42)
set a match: 21 (1.2.109)
set off his head: 116 (5.1.88)
setter: 44 (2.2.50)
shadow of succession: 86 (3.2.99); 147
shape of likelihood: 15 (1.1.58); 136
shot-free: 123 (5.2.130)
shotten herring: 56 (2.4.131)
sinew: 111 (4.4.17)
sirrah: 24 (1.2.183); 139
skimble-skamble: 78 (3.1.154)
slip: 36 (1.3.276)
smug: 76 (3.1.103)
sneak-up: 93 (3.3.87)

snuff: 27 (1.3.41)
so (provided that): 34 (1.3.206)
so (very well): 117 (5.1.122)
soothers: 98 (4.1.7)
soul: 99 (4.1.50)
soused gurnet: 103 (4.2.12)
sovereign'st: 28 (1.3.57)
speed: 79 (3.1.190)
spleen: 50 (2.3.79)
squire: 42 (2.2.13)
stand the push: 85 (3.2.66)
standing-tuck: 60 (2.4.252)
starling: 34 (1.3.224)
start of spleen: 87 (3.2.125)
starting-hole: 61 (2.4.267)
starved: 39 (2.1.27)
state: 65 (2.4.383)
stay (await): 36 (1.3.25.)
stay (linger): 106 (4.2.77)
still: 36 (1.3.276)
stirring: 46 (2.2.99)
stockfish: 60 (2.4.250)
stole: 84 (3.2.50); 147
stomach: 48 (2.3.42)
stout: 129 (5.3.93)
straight: 30 (1.3.126)
strait: 109 (4.3.79)
strappado: 60 (2.4.242); 143
stronds: 13 (1.1.4); 135
subornation: 32 (1.3.163)
suddenly: 37 (1.3.292)
sue his livery: 108 (4.3.62)
sufferances: 115 (5.1.51)
suggestion: 108 (4.3.51)
suits: 20 (1.2.74)
sullen: 25 (1.2.218)
summer-house: 78 (3.1.164)
superfluous: 18 (1.2.11)
suspicion: 119 (5.2.8); 150
Sutton Cophill: 103 (4.2.3); 149
sweet tale of the sun's: 56 (2.4.123); 143
sword-and-buckler: 35 (1.3.230)

tailor: 82 (3.1.261); 147
take it upon: 52 (2.4.9)
take me with you: 68 (2.4.465)
taken with the manner: 63 (2.4.320)
tall: 28 (1.3.62)
tallow-catch: 60 (2.4.233)
target: 59 (2.4.206)
task me to my word: 98 (4.1.9)
task'd: 109 (4.3.92)
tasking: 120 (5.2.50)
tench: 39 (2.1.15); 141

Index of Words Glossed

termagant: 130 (5.3.114); 151
that: 84 (3.2.48,70)
they: 128 (5.3.80)
tickle-brain: 66 (2.4.402); 144
time: 84 (3.2.36)
tinker: 52 (2.4.19); 142
Titan: 56 (2.4.121); 143
tithe: 92 (3.3.60); 148
toss: 105 (4.2.65)
tottered: 104 (4.2.34)
touch: 111 (4.4.10)
trace: 74 (3.1.48)
tranquillity: 41 (2.1.76); 141
trenching: 13 (1.1.7)
trim: 102 (4.1.113)
tripartite: 75 (3.1.81)
tristful: 66 (2.4.398)
triumph: 91 (3.3.42)
Trojans: 41 (2.1.69)
truncheon: 93 (3.3.89)
trunk of humors: 68 (2.4.454)
Turk Gregory: 124 (5.2.145); 151
twelve score: 72 (2.4.554)

underskinker: 52 (2.4.24)
uneven: 15 (1.1.50)
unsorted: 47 (2.3.12)
unwashed hands: 96 (3.3.190); 148
unyok'd: 25 (1.2.202)
uttered: 17 (1.1.107); 137

valors: 133 (5.4.29)
valued: 89 (3.2.177)
vassal: 87 (3.2.124)
velvet-guards: 82 (3.1.258); 147

vile: 86 (3.2.87)
virtue: 56 (2.4.120)
vizards: 22 (1.2.130)

wait on us: 117 (5.1.111)
wan: 85 (3.2.59)
wandering knight: 18 (1.2.15); 137
want: 99 (4.1.44)
wanton: 80 (3.1.214)
wanton time: 115 (5.1.50)
ward: 59 (2.4.198)
wards: 24 (1.2.194)
warm: 103 (4.2.17)
water-colors: 116 (5.1.80)
watering: 52 (2.4.16)
waylaid: 23 (1.2.167)
weaver: 56 (2.4.134); 143
well-respected: 106 (4.3.10)
well said: 128 (5.3.75)
Welsh hook: 64 (2.4.343)
which: 17 (1.1.98)
whoreson: 45 (2.2.84)
wild: 40 (2.1.55)
wilful-blame: 78 (3.1.177)
wind: 102 (4.1.109)
wing: 84 (3.2.30)
withers: 38 (2.1.7)
worship: 88 (3.2.151)
wrung: 38 (2.1.6)

yeomen's: 103 (4.2.15)
York: 35 (1.3.245); 140
younker: 92 (3.3.82)
your . . . your: 39 (2.1.20)

'Zounds: 21 (1.2.103)